S0-ART-706

TWENTY-FOUR EYES

TWENTY-FOUR EYES

by
SAKAE TSUBOI

translated by
AKIRA MIURA

CHARLES E. TUTTLE COMPANY
Rutland, Vermont & Tokyo, Japan

Representatives

Continental Europe: BOXERBOOKS, INC., Zurich

British Isles: PRENTICE-HALL INTERNATIONAL, INC., London

Australasia: BOOK WISE (AUSTRALIA) PTY. LTD.
104-108 Sussex Street, Sydney 2000

Published by the Charles E. Tuttle Company, Inc.
of Rutland, Vermont & Tokyo, Japan
with editorial offices at
Suido 1-chome, 2-6, Bunkyo-ku, Tokyo, Japan

© 1983 by Charles E. Tuttle Co., Inc.

All rights reserved

Library of Congress Catalog Card No. 82-51098
International Standard Book No. 0-8048-1462-7

Originally published in Japanese as *Nijushi no Hitomi*
by Kobunsha, Tokyo in 1952
© 1952 by Sakae Tsuboi
First Tuttle edition, 1983
Second printing, 1985

PRINTED IN JAPAN

Preface

Sakae Tsuboi, the authoress, was born in Shodo Island in the Seto Inland Sea in 1900. After finishing grade school, she worked as a clerk at the post office and the village office of the island for about ten years. In 1925, she moved to Tokyo, where she married Shigeji Tsuboi, a poet. Later she became acquainted with women novelists, such as Yuriko Miyamoto and Ineko Sata, and through their encouragement she started writing fiction.

Since the war, she has produced a number of novels. It is generally known that she is particularly adept at stories of which the principal characters are children. For some of the works of this kind she has won literary prizes.

Nijushi no Hitomi, or *Twenty-four Eyes*, was published in 1952 and immediately became a best seller. Shortly afterward it was made into a film by movie director Keisuke Kinoshita and was enthusiastically received by people of all ages.

Twenty-four Eyes, as you will see, is an anti-war novel. The reader, however, should not expect from this story a complete elucidation of pacifism. Such issues as

" What causes war? ", " How can we prevent war? " and " Are all wars unjustifiable? ", for instance, are hardly touched on in this book.   Sakae Tsuboi merely points out, by following the growth of twelve innocent children, the cruelty and inhumanity of modern warfare.   Hers may be a rather naive kind of pacifism based simply on hatred of war and love of humanity, but precisely for that reason she succeeded in making *Twenty-four Eyes* a touching and convincing novel.

Acknowledgments

I should like to acknowledge here my indebtedness to those whom I owe the completion of this translation. I am particularly grateful to David and Sally McGrath, who, by kindly correcting this book in manuscript form, helped make my English less awkward than it otherwise would have been. Others who have given me many useful suggestions are Robert Jacobs, Emily Potter, and Robert Schmalzried. My thanks are also due to Professor Donald Keene, who offered me invaluable hints which helped me in the translation.

Next I wish to express my appreciation to those whose good offices made the publication of this book possible. Among these are Professor Rikutaro Fukuda and Professor Shigehiko Toyama. I am also indebted to Mr. and Mrs. Tsuboi for permitting me to translate this novel, and to Kenkyusha, especially to Mr. Torao Ueda of the Publishing Department.

Lastly I extend my sincerest thanks to Professor Junsaku Ozawa, without whose sympathetic aid this translation would not have appeared in book form.

AKIRA MIURA

Tokyo

Contents

The Names of Miss Oishi's
Twelve Pupils

GIRLS

Kotsuru Kabe, the talkative daughter of a " bellman."

Masuno Kagawa, the musically-talented daughter of a restaurant keeper.

Kotoe Katagiri, the daughter of a fisherman.

Matsue (Matchan) Kawamoto, the daughter of a carpenter.

Fujiko Kinoshita, the daughter of a squire.

Misako (Miisan) Nishiguchi, the daughter of a well-to-do family.

Sanae Yamaishi, a shy yet bright girl.

BOYS

Nita Aizawa, a talkative boy with a loud voice.

Isokichi (Sonki) Okada, the son of a bean-curd dealer.

Tadashi (Tanko) Morioka, the son of a head fisherman.

Takeichi Takeshita, the bright son of a rice dealer.

Kichiji (Kitchin) Tokuda, a quiet boy.

TWENTY-FOUR EYES

1

Miss Koishi

If, as they say, twenty years make a generation, this story began a little more than a generation ago. As for the memorable events of the time, the electoral system had just been revised, and the first election under the new Universal Suffrage Law had taken place in February. Two months after this election, on the fourth of April, 1928, a young woman arrived to teach school at a humble village on the Inland Sea, a farming and fishing community.

The village numbered only slightly more than a hundred families and was situated at the tip of a long cape that made the bay appear to be a lake. The villagers, therefore, had either to go by rowboat or to walk around by the long, winding path through the hills to visit the towns and villages across the bay.

Because the village was so isolated, the children of primary school age attended a branch school there for their first four years. When they reached the fifth grade, they were allowed for the first time to go to the school in the principal village three miles away. Their handmade straw sandals wore out each day, but the children were proud of this. How glad they must have been to wear new sandals every morning! In the fifth grade they began making their own sandals, too. It was fun to gather at someone's house on Sundays to make sandals. While they enviously watched the older ones, the younger children would learn the art without consciously trying. For the little children, growing up to be fifth graders was like becoming independent. Still the branch school was not without its share of fun.

The branch school had always had two teachers: a very old man and a very young woman. It had been that way since long ago, as though there had been a regulation about it. The old man lived in the night duty room next to the faculty room, while the young woman came from a long way off to school every day. The old man would teach the third and fourth graders, while the young woman taught the first and second grades. All this had long been common practice. The children called their teachers " Gentleman Teacher " and " Lady Teacher " instead of calling them by their names. The old man would settle down, hoping to retire eventually on a pension, while the young woman would leave after a year—or two at the most. It was said that the branch school on the cape was a place where men teachers with no hope to be principals spent the rest of their working days, and where the new women teachers got their first hard experiences. This was only rumor, of course, and could not be proven, but it was probably true all the same.

Now, let us go back to the fourth of April, 1928. That morning, the pupils, fifth grade and up, from the cape village were happily walking their three miles to the main school. They were all so happy to have been promoted to higher grades that their steps were light. The textbooks in their bags were all new, and the prospect of being taught by new teachers in new classrooms made them feel as though they were indeed marching over new roads. Besides, today they were looking forward to meeting on the way the new woman teacher who was coming to the branch school in their village for the first time.

"I wonder what kind of a dame the new Lady Teacher'll be," said one of the boys of the upper grade school who would have been of about the same age as today's junior high school students. He used the rude word purposely.

"They say this new one's just out of girls' high school, too."

"Then she'll only be half-baked again, won't she?"

"After all, our village always gets half-baked teachers."

"Poor villages have to put up with them."

Teachers who graduated from girls' high school only, rather than from regular teachers' colleges—perhaps they would be called assistant teachers now—, were called half-baked by evil-tongued grown-ups. These boys were mimicking them, pretending to be adults themselves. But they were not particularly malicious. The fifth graders who joined the upper-class pupils for the first time today, however, could only blink in astonishment and listen modestly, as newcomers would. Yet it was the fifth graders who first shouted with joy when they caught sight of a figure coming toward them.

"Hurrah! Lady Teacher!"

It was Miss Kobayashi who had been teaching at the branch school until just recently. Usually she only made some brief response to the bows of the pupils as she passed them, but today she stopped and looked fondly at one face after another.

"Today is really the last day. I'm afraid we won't be meeting any more on this road. I hope you'll all be good pupils."

Some of the girls were quite moved, and their eyes filled with tears. Miss Kobayashi had replaced a teacher who had quit because of illness. Yet unlike all the former women teachers, she had stayed at the branch school three and a half years. Therefore, the children she met on the path today had all once been her own pupils. According to custom, changes in the faculty were not announced until the first day of a new term, but Miss Kobayashi had defied this tradition and had told her pupils ten days in advance. On their way back from the closing ceremony at the main school on the 25th of March, they had met her just where they were now standing, and she had made her farewells to them and given each a box of caramels. That was why they had been expecting today to see the new teacher coming their way. But Miss Kobayashi had come along first, to their surprise. Probably Miss Kobayashi was on her way to say good-by to the branch school pupils today.

" Miss Kobayashi, where's the new teacher? "

" I guess she'll be along pretty soon."

" What's she like? "

" I don't know yet."

" Just out of high school again? "

" I really don't know. Anyway, don't any of you be mean to her," said Miss Kobayashi with a smile. She, too, used to be teased by the children on her way to school during her first year and had been made to cry, sometimes even right in front of them. Those who had made her cry were not among the group today ; they were the older brothers and sisters of the children who were there. Most of the women teachers who came to the cape were made to cry at least once because they were young and inexperienced, and the children here knew this almost as a tradition. They were full of curiosity about the newcomer especially because Miss Kobayashi had been at the branch school so long. After they left her, they planned their tactics, all the while looking ahead, expecting at any moment to see the new teacher approaching them.

" Shall we shout ' Potato girl ! ' ? "

" What if she isn't a potato girl? "

" I'm sure she will be, though."

In that part of the country, sweet potatoes were grown in great abundance, and there was a girls' school right in the middle of the sweet potato fields. Miss Kobayashi was a graduate of that *potato school*, and the children took it for granted that the new teacher, too, would have come from the same place. They craned their necks at every bend in the path, expecting to see her. But, without encountering this much-awaited new teacher fresh from the potato school, they finally arrived at the wide prefectural road that led to the principal village. At once, they forgot all about her and started running, because the big clock in the hall of the inn on the prefectural road, which they customarily looked at, was ten minutes past the usual time. The clock was not ten minutes fast, but they had stopped ten minutes with Miss Kobayashi. They all went on running, raising the dust, their school bags rattling on their backs or tucked under their arms.

They did not think of the new teacher again until they were on their way home in the afternoon and had arrived at the path that branched off toward the cape from the prefectual road. Again, they saw Miss Kobayashi coming toward them. Miss Kobayashi, in her long-sleeved kimono, was moving her hands in a peculiar way, fluttering her sleeves.

" Teacher ! "

" Lady Teacher ! "

All the girls started running. As Miss Kobayashi's smiling face drew nearer and more distinct, the children realized that she was pretending to pull an invisible rope with both her hands, and they all laughed. She moved her hands alternately as though she were actually gathering in a rope, till at last she stopped and hauled them all in around her.

" Miss Kobayashi, did the new teacher come ? "

" Yes. Why ? "

" Is she still at the school ? "

" Oh, that's it, is it ? She came by boat today."

" She did ? And did she go home by boat too ? "

" Yes, she asked me to take the boat with her, but I said No, because I wanted to see you again."

" Oh, boy ! " the girls shouted with joy, while the boys watched them, grinning. Then, one of the boys asked, " What kind of a teacher is she? "

" She seems like a very nice teacher. She's awfully pretty," answered Miss Kobayashi, looking as though she had just remembered the fact.

" Is she a potato girl? "

" No, no, she's much better than that."

" But she's green, isn't she? "

Suddenly Miss Kobayashi looked angry and said, " Why do you say that when she's not even your teacher? Besides, there's no such thing as a teacher who's not green at first. You mean to make her cry the way I was made to cry, don't you? "

Some looked away at the tone of her voice, knowing that she read their minds correctly. At the time Miss Kobayashi was first appointed to the branch school, the older pupils used to tease her in all sorts of ways. They would purposely form a line and bow with mock solemnity, or shout " Potato girl! " at her, or stare fixedly or just grin at her. In the course of three and a half years, however, she had become inured, and, no matter what they did, it no longer bothered her. In fact, she sometimes even teased them herself. After all, it was natural for her to want some kind of diversion on her three-mile walk.

After a while, another pupil asked, " What's the new teacher's name? "

" Miss Oishi. But she's very small. I'm tall although I'm a Kobayashi.* But she's really tiny. She comes only to my shoulders."

" Really ? "

When the children laughed as though they were glad, Miss Kobayashi looked serious again.

" But she's much, much better educated than we are. She's not half-trained like me."

"Is that so ? And does she come to school by boat ? " asked one for whom this was evidently a serious problem. Miss Kobayashi, seeing their concern, replied, " No, it was only for today. You'll be meeting her from tomorrow on. But you can't make her cry. I warned her and said, ' You'll meet the main school pupils on your way to and from school, but if they play tricks on you, just pretend they're monkeys playing. If they say nasty things, pretend they're crows cawing.' "

" Gosh ! "

" Goodness ! "

They all laughed, and Miss Kobayashi, too, joined in. Then they parted, but the children continued to call after her in turn until she disappeared around the next bend.

" Teacher ! "

---

* The teacher was making a play on words from the meanings of their names ; " Oishi " means " big stone " while " Kobayashi " means " small wood."

" Good-by ! "

" Miss Bride-to-be ! "

" Good-by ! "

They already knew that Miss Kobayashi had resigned because she was going to be married soon. When she turned around to wave for the last time and then disappeared, they were left, as might be expected, with a strange, sad feeling in their hearts. Feeling tired, too, after the day's activity, they trudged on with heavy steps. When they arrived home they found the village in a hubbub.

" The new Lady Teacher wears Western clothes ! "

" She isn't a potato girl ! "

" She's so small ! "

The next day, the children excitedly planned tactics to shock this little teacher who was not from the potato school. They were walking to school, whispering to one another. And then they were taken by surprise. The place was unfavorable, too. Near the bend which obstructed the view ahead, a bicycle, a rarity on that path, came suddenly into sight. It was upon them before they realized it, coming swiftly as a bird, and riding it, a woman in Western clothes. She smiled at them, said " Good morning ! " and was gone, like a gust of wind.

She must have been Lady Teacher. They had been prepared for her to come plodding along on foot, and here she had swished past them on a bicycle. This was their first experience of a woman teacher riding a bicycle. Nor had they known a teacher who said " Good morning ! " to them on her first work day. For a while, they just gaped after her. It was a complete defeat for them. She was certainly nothing like any new teacher they had ever seen before. They knew she would not be made to cry by any ordinary mischief.

" She looks pretty tough."

" A woman riding a bike ! "

" Kind of fresh, isn't she ? "

While the boys thus criticized her, the girls also started discussing her with spirit, although from a different point of view, as is usually the case with girls.

" What do you think ? Maybe she's what they call a ' modern girl ' ? "

" But a modern girl has her hair cut short right here like a man, hasn't she ? " replied another, putting two fingers in the shape of scissors behind her ears. " And she had her hair in a bun."

" She's got Western clothes on, though."

" Maybe her family runs a bicycle store, and that's why she's riding such a nice bike. It certainly was shiny."

" I wish we could ride bikes too. It must be wonderful to ride along this road so fast."

How were they to compete with this bicycle? No doubt they all felt discouraged as though they had been ignominiously thrown in a judo match. Everyone was trying in his own way to think of ways to get the better of her. Before they could think of anything, however, they came to the end of the cape path. Once again, the clock in the hall of the inn told them they were late, by almost eight minutes. They set off with a rush; the pencil cases on their backs and under their arms began clattering all at once, and the dust rose in clouds from under their straw sandals.

At just about the same time, the villagers on the cape were also making a great fuss. The village wives had heard about the teacher having come by boat yesterday and gone back the same way without their knowing it. Today they were all the more curious about her since they had heard she wore Western clothes, wondering how she would look as she passed by. Particularly, the proprietress of the general store, at the entrance of the village, which was nicknamed the " Checking Station," had been watching the street since the break of dawn, as though she had the right to see whoever came to the cape village before anybody else. Since it had not rained for quite some time, she thought it would be a good idea to sprinkle water on the dusty street for the new teacher. Just as she got outside with her bucket, however, a bicycle came speeding along. Before she knew what was happening, the woman on it passed by with a friendly bow and a " Good morning ! "

" Good morning," answered the proprietress, when it suddenly dawned on her who it was. But the bicycle was already going down the slope which began right there. She ran to the carpenter's next door in a great hurry and shouted at his wife who was soaking her washing by the well.

" Listen, listen ! A girl in Western clothes just went by on a bike ! Was it Lady Teacher, do you think ? "

" Was she wearing a white shirt and a black jacket like a man's ? "

" Yup, she was."

" Good gracious ! On a bike, you said ? " exclaimed the carpenter's wife, forgetting the washing ; yesterday she had taken her oldest daughter, Matsue, to school for the entrance ceremony. The proprietress looked as though she entirely agreed with the other. " The world has really changed. A woman teacher riding a bike ! I'm afraid she'll be called forward," she said in a worried voice, but the look in her eyes revealed that she was already convinced the girl *was* forward.

Less than fifteen minutes after the bicycle swished past the general store, from which the school was only a few minutes' ride, the rumor about Lady

Teacher had spread all over the village. The pupils at school were in an uproar, too. Less than fifty in number altogether, they were standing around the bicycle by the entrance of the faculty room, jabbering as noisily as quarreling sparrows. Yet, when Lady Teacher approached them to talk, they scattered like frightened sparrows. When she reluctantly went back into the faculty room, she found Gentleman Teacher, her only colleague, sitting silently with a completely unsympathetic look. Behind the cabinet on his desk, he was reading some papers, with his head down, as though he would hate to be spoken to. Since she had finished talking over her duties there yesterday, when Miss Kobayashi had transferred all the business to her, there was nothing particular left to be discussed. But all the same, she complained to herself, Gentleman Teacher was too unfriendly. As for him, however, he had his own troubles.

"What shall I do? A fully-qualified teacher fresh from the women teachers' college looks quite different from a half-trained teacher just out of the potato school. She's very small, but she looks bright. I wonder if we've got anything in common to talk about. I thought she was pretty modern because she came in Western clothes yesterday. But I didn't expect her to come on a bicyle. What shall I do? Why in the world did they send over such a first-rate woman this time? What's the matter with the principal anyway?"

His heart was heavy with these thoughts. He was a farmer's son who had spent ten years preparing for the examination for a teachers' license and finally he had become fully qualified about four or five years ago; he was more industrious than gifted. He always wore wooden clogs, and his only suit had discolored around the shoulders. He had no children and lived a frugal life with his old wife, taking pleasure only in saving money. He was so peculiar that he accepted the kind of assignment others would have shunned, and had gladly come to this isolated cape village, because he thought he would not need to be sociable there. He put his shoes on only when he went to the main school, for instance, to attend faculty meetings; as for bicycles, he had never even touched one. But he was well liked in the village so that he was never in need of fish or vegetables. For this man, who was as dirty as the villagers, ate the same food they ate, and spoke their language, the Western clothes and the bicycle of the newly-arrived Lady Teacher were a cause of great embarrassment.

However, she did not suspect anything of that sort. She had heard from her predecessor, Miss Kobayashi, about the mischievous pupils attending the main school. As to Gentleman Teacher, Miss Kobayashi had merely whispered to her, "A peculiar person.

Never mind him." But to her he looked more mean than peculiar, and she was afraid she might unconsciously give a sigh even though it was only her second day.

Her name was Hisako Oishi. She had been born in the village with the tall solitary pine tree across the lake-like bay. From the cape village the pine looked as small as a dwarf tree. In her house by the tree, her mother, all alone, must be thinking of her, wondering if she was doing all right at school. When she thought of that, the tiny Miss Oishi felt like expanding her chest and drawing in a deep breath to call aloud " Mother ! " from the bottom of her heart.

A little while ago, the principal, a friend of her deceased father's, had said, " I'm awfully sorry the cape is such a long way off. But will you please put up with it just for a year? I'll call you back to the main school later. It's better to have a hard time at the branch school first."

Heeding these words, Miss Oishi had decided to accept the job, hoping it would be over in a year. She had been advised to rent a room there, because the school was too far to walk to, but she had thought of her mother, from whom she had lived apart for the past two years, while attending the teachers' school attached to the municipal girls' school. All that time, their sole consolation had lain in the hope that they

could live together afterwards. Therefore she made
up her mind to go to school by bicycle every day
even though it was five miles away. She had bought
the bicycle through a good friend of hers, a bicycle
dealer's daughter, on the five-month installment plan.
Since she had not any presentable clothes, she had had
her mother's serge kimono dyed black and had made,
though clumsily, a suit out of it herself. People who
did not know anything about these things may have
thought that she was forward because she rode a
bicycle, and stylish because she wore Western clothes.
After all, it was 1928. Moreover, the village was such
an isolated place that the general election, which had
just taken place, was considered something foreign.
Because the bicycle was new and bright and the black
hand-sewn suit was not dirty, and because the white
blouse was pure white, she probably looked extremely
extravagant, forward, and unapproachable to the villagers on the cape. But how could she guess all these
things on her second day at her new post? She felt
as lonely and lost as if she had come to a foreign country
where she could not make herself understood; so she
just looked at the pine tree, thinking of her home
close by it.

Click-clack! click-clack! went the thwacking board
to mark the beginning of school, shocking Miss Oishi
out of her reverie. The boy standing on tiptoes,

striking the board, had yesterday been elected president of the fourth grade, which was the highest in the school. When she went out into the playground, Miss Oishi noticed that the group of first graders was in a peculiar, silent turmoil; one could sense in them both pride and a kind of anxiety because they had come to school for the first time by themselves today, leaving their parents behind.

After the third and fourth graders went quickly into their classroom, Miss Oishi beat time with her hands for a while, making her pupils keep time with their feet; then, walking backwards, she led them into the classroom. At last she began to feel more self-confident and relaxed. When they sat down, she came down from the platform with the roll in her hand.

" Now," she said, " when your name's called, please answer loudly.—Master Isokichi Okada ! "

Because they were seated in order of height, Isokichi Okada, being a small boy, was in the first row. He was not only embarrassed because his name was called first, but was taken aback to be called " Master " for the first time in his life. His answer stuck in his throat.

" Isn't Master Isokichi Okada present? "

As she looked around, a huge boy in the back row answered in a surprisingly loud voice, " He is."

" Please say ' Present ' then. Master Isokichi Okada!" Looking at the big boy who had answered, she approached his seat, when the second graders burst into laughter. The real Isokichi Okada was standing embarrassed.

"Sonki, answer now," urged a second grade girl in a low voice, who looked very much like him. Probably it was his sister.

"Do you call him Sonki?" asked the teacher. They all nodded together.

"I see. Then Sonki, short for Isokichi!"

Everyone laughed again. Laughing with them, she put down the nickname in the roll with her pencil in small letters.

"Next, Master Takeichi Takeshita!"

"Present," answered a bright-looking boy.

"That's it. Your answer was nice and clear.— Next, Master Kichiji Tokuda!"

While Kichiji took a little pause to inhale, the boy who had said "He is," about Isokichi a minute ago, took the opportunity to shout "Kitchin!" a little impudently. He, Nita Aizawa by name, became even more impudent when everyone burst out laughing again, and he shouted "Tanko!" when the next name, Tadashi Morioka, was called. When his own turn came, he answered even more loudly, "PRESENT!"

The teacher said a bit reproachfully, though with

a smile, " You're minding other people's business a little too much, Master Nita Aizawa. Your voice is too loud, too. From now, when I call somebody's name, I want him to answer himself.—Miss Matsue Kawamoto ! "

" Present."

" What do they call you? "

" Matchan."

" I see. Is your father a carpenter? "

Matsue nodded.

" Miss Misako Nishiguchi ! "

" Present."

" Your nickname must be Misachan."

The girl shook her head, however, and said in a low voice, " They call me Miisan."

" Oh, Miisan? Isn't that cute ! —Next, Miss Masuno Kagawa ! "

" Yeah."

Miss Oishi almost burst out laughing, but managed not to. Stifling a laugh, she said, " 'Yeah' sounds a little funny. Let's say 'Present,' Masuno."

Then Nita, the meddler, cut in again, " It's Mahchan ! "

She paid him no more attention but kept on calling one name after another.

" Miss Fujiko Kinoshita ! "

" Present."

" Miss Sanae Yamaishi ! "

" Present."

Miss Oishi smiled at each child as the answer was given.

" Miss Kotsuru Kabe ! "

Suddenly they all became noisy. At first, she was surprised, not knowing what was the matter, but when she understood what they were all saying, the young teacher found it funnier than Masuno's " Yeah," and finally burst out laughing. They were saying, " Kotsuru Kabe, Kotsuru Kabe, rub the wall with your head ! "*

Kotsuru Kabe, who seemed to be a girl who hated to give in, did not cry, but sat blushing, with her head down. By the time the noise had quieted down and the last name, Kotoe Katagiri, had been called, the forty-five minutes' class time was already up. Before school was over that day, Miss Oishi fixed in her memory that Kotsuru Kabe was the daughter of a "bellman" (a man with a bell attached to his belt who did all sorts of errands); that Fujiko Kinoshita came of an old family; that Masuno Kagawa, who answered " Yeah," was the daughter of a restaurant keeper in town; that the family of Isokichi Okada, Sonki for short, ran a bean-curd store; and that Tadashi

---

* " Kotsuru " sounds similar to the word meaning " rub," while " Kabe " sounds like the word for " wall."

Morioka, or Tanko, was the son of a head fisherman. Though their fathers were called bean-curd dealers, rice dealers, or head fishermen by trade, none of them could make a living by his respective business alone. Consequently, in their spare time, all of them were also farmers and fishermen. In that respect, this village was the same as Miss Oishi's. It was a village where everyone had to work without a minute's leisure. But by looking at their faces, you could tell that they did not mind working at all.

All these children, who were starting today to learn the three R's from the very beginning, would do baby-sitting, help their families husk wheat, or go out to draw in the nets as soon as they got home. Miss Oishi wondered how she could get along with them, the children in this poor village, where work seemed the only object in life. At that moment, she was only ashamed to think how sentimental she had been to look at the Pine Tree with tears in her eyes. Just finished with her first experience of teaching, she thought of the twelve first graders who had tasted group life for the first time that day. She saw their eyes vividly, each pair shining with its own individuality. " Never in the world will I disillusion those eyes," she told herself.

That afternoon, as she pedalled over the five-mile road back to her village, Miss Oishi's high spirits made her seem even more forward to the villagers than she had in the morning.

" Good-by ! "

" Good-by ! "

" Good-by ! "

She greeted everyone she rode past, but not many responded. The few who did merely nodded. It was no wonder, for she was already a target of criticism in the village.

" She even put down their nicknames in the roll, I hear."

" They say she called Misako Nishiguchi cute."

" She's prejudiced already, isn't she? Maybe the Nishiguchis gave her a present or something to butter her up."

Riding along lightly in complete ignorance of what was going on, the small Miss Oishi came as far as the slope at the edge of the village. Then, bending forward a little and putting her strength into her feet, she rode on, wanting to tell her mother about her enthusiasm as soon as she could. The slope, although gentle enough for walkers, had been a source of pleasant speed on her way to school; on her way home now, it was a handicap. But she felt so happy and grateful that she did not mind that the slope was not the other way round.

When she reached the top of the slope, she saw

the group of pupils she had met in the morning.

" Oishi, Koishi ! "

" Oishi, Koishi ! "

The chorus became louder and louder as her bicycle approached them with increasing speed. At first, she could not make it out. But when she understood that it referred to herself, she involuntarily laughed aloud, for she realized that it was her new nickname. She purposely rang the bell loudly and shouted, as she went by, " Good-by now ! "

They gave a shout of joy and kept on calling " Oishi, Koishi ! " which became less and less audible behind her back.

Thus she acquired the name " Miss Koishi " in addition to " Lady Teacher " that day. It was because she was small, she thought. With the setting sun shining dazzlingly bright on her new bicycle, Miss Koishi continued her way along the cape road.

2

A Magic Bridge

Near the middle of the narrow, two-and-a-half-mile cape, there was another little hamlet. The white path along the bay turned at this point and crossed the cape. It then followed the shore line overlooking the open sea, to the cape school village. Every morning, she met the pupils going to the main school, almost invariably just about where the road began to run along the ocean. If they met at the wrong place, even just a short distance from the usual spot, one of the two parties had to hurry up. Ordinarily, it was the pupils. They would shout "Golly, Miss Ko-ishi's coming!" and suddenly quickened their pace. But, occasionally, the teacher caught sight of them coming toward her while she was still riding along the bay side, and began to pedal harder. How glad the pupils were in a case like that! They would jeer at her, as she rode by with her face glowing.

"Hey, fine thing for a teacher to be late!"

"We'll cut your pay!"

There were even some who did naughty things in her path as she came. One day, after a long series of such mischief, she complained to her mother about it when she got home.

"Can you imagine such little kids having the nerve to shout, 'We'll cut your pay!'? They're too interested in things like money. Isn't it disgusting?"

Her mother smiled and said, "Don't be silly. You shouldn't mind that sort of thing. Anyway, it's only for a year. Patience, patience."

Actually, Miss Oishi did not need her mother's encouragement, for she was not hurt that much. As she got used to it, she came to enjoy the five miles' bicycle ride in the early morning more than she had expected. About the time she was crossing the cape, her bicycle would begin to go faster, and, before she knew it, she would be racing the children. Naturally, that in turn affected the pupils and caused them to quicken their pace, too.

The first term passed while Miss Oishi and the pupils were competing in this kind of seesaw game. One day, Gentleman Teacher went to the main school on business and returned with the strange news that the children from the cape had never been late for school during the past term. Everyone knew that to cover the three miles' distance was not easy. Consequently, since long ago, the cape children had always been excused for not being on time. But if, on the contrary, they had not been late for school even once, they certainly deserved commendation. And, of course, it was praised as a great deed. Gentleman Teacher was as glad as if he had brought it about himself.

"One of this year's pupils is very exceptional. That must be why," he said, thinking the thirty boys and girls from the cape had not been late for school just because of one particular fifth grade girl who had done excellently even in competition with all the pupils of the main school. Actually, it was due to Lady Teacher's bicycle. But she did not realize it, either. Instead, she was often touched by the diligence of the cape village children and thought she should put up with such things as their mischief. At the same time, she secretly applauded her own diligence, too.

"I was late only once myself, when my bike had a flat tire on the way. Besides, I have to cover five miles one way," she said to herself. Looking out of the window, she thought of her mother, who always gave her so much encouragement. The calm bay glittered in the sun, as on a typical summer day, and the Pine Tree village, where her mother was, looked hazy under the white summer clouds. From the wide-open window, the sea breeze blew in, filling her whole being with the joyful expectation of the summer vacation starting in two more days. Yet she still felt a little unhappy about the villagers, who would not open their hearts to her. When she complained to Gentleman Teacher about them, he said, laughing with his mouth wide open, showing his missing back teeth, " That's expecting too much. You see, however often you visit their homes, you can't make friends as long as you wear Western clothes and ride a bike. The people feel awkward because you're a little too modern. It's the way this village is."

Lady Teacher was taken aback. She blushed and thought over his words with her head down. " Does he mean I should walk to school in a kimono? It's a ten-mile round trip. . . ."

She thought it over several times during the summer vacation, but before she could bring herself to change her mind, the second term came. Even though the calendar said September, she was still afraid of the effect of the heat, after the long vacation. The small Lady Teacher had lost a little weight and was rather pale.

The first morning of the new term, as she was leaving her house, her mother said, " After all, one third of the year is over. Patience, patience, just for a little while longer."

With these words of encouragement, she helped her daughter get the bicycle out. Miss Oishi, though a teacher, was human, too, and sometimes she spoke to her mother like a spoiled child.

" Oh—patience, patience. Bother ! " she retorted and started off on her bicycle quickly, as if she were angry. Riding fast through the air for the first time in many weeks, she was permeated with a pleasant feeling. On the other hand, the thought of bicycling to school again from today on depressed her. During the vacation she had talked with her mother about it several times. She had discussed the possibility of renting a room on the cape, but finally had decided to keep on going by bicycle. It was pleasant riding in the morning, but riding back in the afternoon with the scorching heat reflecting from the surface of the road, and the setting sun beating down on her back, was so enervating that it was sometimes difficult to breathe. She could see the cape village right before her eyes. Wasn't it a shame, she thought to herself, that she had to take the trouble day after day to go all the way around the bay? What was worse, the people on the cape did not like her bicycle !

" Dammit ! " She did not really say it, but unconsciously she was putting more strength into her feet when she looked at the cape lying ahead. On her right, the bay looked unusually rough. While she was still riding in the opposite direction from the tip of the cape, it suddenly occurred to her that today was the first day of the typhoon season, according to the calendar. She realized then that the wind was blowing unusually hard against her cheeks, filling the air with the smell of the sea. The tops of the hills on the cape appeared to be shaking slightly, making her realize how rough the open sea must be. She was becoming a little anxious. She might even have to get off the bicycle before she got there. In that case, the bicycle would be more of a burden than anything else. She told herself that it was too late to get off now anyway. Her thoughts flew about like birds.

" ' Calm down, wind ! ' I order like Ali Baba. Suddenly the wind drops, and the sea becomes unbelievably quiet. It's as calm as a lake very early in the morning. ' Span the bay, bridge ! ' I point with my forefinger. All of a sudden, there's a bridge over the water, a fine bridge as beautiful as a rainbow. Only *I* can see it and cross it. I ride slowly, because it would be awful if I fell into the sea. Even though I take my time crossing the arching, rainbow-colored bridge, yet I reach the cape village forty-five minutes early. How surprised they all are ! When they see me, the villagers hastily put their clocks forty-five minutes forward. I feel sorry to see the children in a panic ; they choke down their breakfasts and dash out of their houses before they have even finished eating. Gentleman Teacher has just gotten up when I get to school. Astonished, he runs to the well and starts washing his face. As for his old wife, she doesn't even have time to change her dress. She fans the charcoal stove desperately, adjusting her nightdress with one hand. She gives me a bashful, awkward smile and rubs the corners of her eyes and mouth a little. She has bad eyes, and her eyes are always only half open in the morning."

The last sentence alone was so true that Miss Oishi let slip a chuckle, but just then her reverie evaporated like a mist. From ahead of her, hindered by the wind, she heard voices calling as before, " Miss Koishi! "

Hearing their familiar call for the first time in a month, she suddenly felt strong and shouted " Y-e-s ! " But the wind seemed to carry her voice backward. As she had expected, the open sea was rough with high waves, and looked as it usually did on a typhoon day.

" You're late today, aren't you? Probably about forty-five minutes late," she said.

The children had stopped to speak to her, with a look that told how much they had missed her; but when they heard her say this, they took her seriously and started running. Miss Oishi, too, rode on harder against the wind. Occasionally eddies of wind would come from nowhere, making her get off the bicycle. It looked as though she really would be about forty-five minutes late. Her own village, with the Pine Tree, lay on the seashore, too. But because it was always protected by the cape, it usually remained safe from

typhoons. On the contrary, the village on the narrow
cape always seemed to be hit on the ocean side and
suffer considerable damage each time. She picked
her way, on her bicycle, along the road which was
scattered with small branches and twigs torn from the
trees. Perhaps she pushed the bicycle more than
she rode it. In this way, she really got to the village
very late. Coming to a place where she had a view
of the whole village, she involuntarily stopped and
exclaimed " Heavens ! "

There was a little wharf at the near end of the village. Near the beginning of the wharf, a fishing boat
lay upside down, its bottom looking like the back
of a whale. Several other boats which apparently
could not be brought in to the wharf had been tossed
up on the road. The road was filled with gravel
washed ashore by the waves and was in no condition
for a bicycle to get through. The village looked like
an entirely different place. Tiles on the roofs of the
houses along the beach had been ripped off. People
were on the roofs reparing them. They all were too
busy to greet the teacher. As for her, she had to push
her bicycle, avoiding the stones cast upon the road,
and in this way she finally reached the school. When
she passed through the gate, the first graders ran up
and surrounded her, their eyes dancing. They were
excited as if they had been glad about the storm that

had visited them the night before. They all started speaking at once in shrill voices, but Masuno Kagawa, being a little forward, outdid the others with her particularly loud voice, as though she believed that she was the only one fit to make a report.

" Teacher," she cried out with her thin-lipped mouth. " Sonki's house was knocked down, like a crab that's been squashed."

At this, the teacher's eyes widened with apprehension. Turning slightly pale, she exclaimed, " Oh, Sonki! Is your family all right? " She looked around and saw the boy nod. He did not seem to have fully recovered from the shock yet.

" Miss Oishi, at my house the well-pole got split, and the big jar by the well broke," said Masuno again.

" How awful! What about the other houses? "

" The general store manager got up on the roof to fix it and fell off! "

" Oh, no! "

" Even at Miisan's, shutters were blown away. Weren't they, Miisan? "

The teacher realized that so far only Masuno had been talking.

" What about the others? Is everything all right? " she asked. Her eyes met those of Sanae Yamaishi, a shy girl, who blushed and nodded. Masuno pulled Miss Oichi's skirt to attract her attention and said,

" Teacher ! There's something more serious. A thief broke into Takeichi's rice store. Isn't that right, Takeichi? You had a bag of rice stolen, didn't you? "

The boy, who was being asked to agree, nodded and answered, " We were careless. We didn't think a thief would come on a stormy night like that. But we got up this morning and found the door of the barn open. Dad said there might be some grains of rice dropped on the road to the thief's house, but he looked and couldn't find any."

" What an awful time you all had ! . . . Excuse me. I must leave my bicycle over there. I'll see you later."

Walking to the faculty room as usual, she suddenly noticed there was more light than usual, and stopped. Once again, she was taken aback. The roof over the well had been blown off; there was nothing left where the familiar tin roof had been. Through the empty space, she saw white clouds floating in the sky.

Gentleman Teacher, with a towel around his head, looked as if he had been bustling about. He spoke to her with unusual cordiality, " Hello, Lady Teacher ! How are you? The storm was pretty wild last night, wasn't it? "

His wife, with her kimono sleeves tied up with a cord, also came out, pulled off the towel from around her head and bowed, asking Lady Teacher how she had been. " The Pine Tree broke, didn't it? " said the old woman.

" What? " Miss Oishi, with a start of surprise, turned her eyes toward her village. The tree still stood right where it should have, but when she looked more carefully, she found it appeared a little different. The storm had not hit her village so hard, but the old pine tree seemed to have had one of its spreading branches ripped off from the trunk by the wind. Even though the damage was slight, she was ashamed that she, who came from that very village, had not noticed it. The old tree had been a landmark to the people who lived on the bay since long ago. What was worse, she had been so impudent early that morning, fancying a magic bridge between the Pine Tree and the cape, and calming the seas with a wave of her arm. Moreover, she had thrown all the villagers into such an uproar that they had put their clocks forty-five minutes forward. And now, having arrived, she found the village in a much greater state of upheaval. Gentleman Teacher was working barefooted instead of washing his face hastily as in her daydream. His wife had long since finished lighting the charcoal stove and was working busily, with her sleeves tucked up.

" Oh, the first day of the second term has begun all wrong," thought Lady Teacher to herself. She remembered with regret how sullen she had been toward her mother when she left the house. When the third period came, she decided, instead of giving a scheduled music lesson, to take the pupils out to inquire after the families that had met misfortune. First she stopped by at Misako Nishiguchi's house, the nearest to the school, and gave her family a word of sympathy. The children told her that Sonki's house, which had collapsed, had suffered by far the greatest damage; so next they made for his house which was on a hill above the village shrine. Miss Oishi remembered how just that morning Masuno had described Sonki's house as a crab that had been squashed. She thought the girl had borrowed the expression from grown-ups; yet, oddly enough, it seemed to arouse a realistic feeling within her. The wreck of the house, however, had been mostly cleared away by the neighbors' helping hands. The storehouse for bean curd, detached from the house, remained standing. Sonki's family had carried their mats in there, put them directly on the dirt floor, and set their household goods upon them. For a while Miss Oishi could not find a word to say, because she felt so sorry, picturing in her mind the whole family of seven sleeping there from tonight on. Matsue Kawamoto's father, who was among the helpers, spoke to her in a joking tone, as carpenters usually do, but not without sarcasm, " Oh, is that you, Lady Teacher? Are you here to help us too? Would you mind getting the whole bunch of kids to roll the stones out of the road down to the beach then? Leave the job here to a carpenter like me. Or would you like to use a hatchet or something?"

The people around him laughed, as if they wanted to make fun of her. She was suddenly embarrassed to realize how carefree she must have appeared to them. But she went on standing there, hoping to give at least a word of sympathy to Sonki's family, because after all that was why she had come. No one paid any attention to her, however. She had to start back, and suggested in order to cover her humiliation, " How about all of us getting the stones out of the road now?"

" Good!"

" Let's!"

At once, the children ran delightedly in all directions. It was one of those hot yet refreshing days that occur after storms. The air was so clear that they could see the whole village from one end to the other.

" Stupid lump!"

" Damn old rocks!"

Everyone, according to his strength, picked up stones and rolled them down to the beach, a few feet below the edge of the road. The road was covered with stones, like a rocky shore. Some of the stones were so big that it took two children to move them. The ocean looked perfectly calm now, the same ocean that had raged so much the previous night, tossing up all these stones over the embankment along the road. It made one marvel at the awful power of nature. It must have been a night of great confusion in the cape village, with the waves carrying up the stones, and the wind blowing the houses down. The teacher was surprised to see how much the cape could do to weaken a storm, sheltering the opposite shore in its lee. She picked up a stone in her arms and heaved it down the beach with force. She asked a third grade boy who was kicking stones out of the road in an experienced manner, " Is this what storms usually do ? "

" Yes."

" And do you clear away stones each time ? "

" Yes."

Just then Masuno Kagawa's mother passed by and said, " Oh, Miss Oishi, aren't you working hard ! You'd better not try to finish it today. I'm sure we have a couple more storms coming very soon."

Masuno's mother, proprietress of a restaurant and inn in town, said she had come to see how everything was on the cape, where her daughter lived. Masuno came running, clung to her, and said, " Mother, I was scared last night. I heard such a big noise I clung to Grandma in bed. This morning we found the well-pole split in half. The jar broke too."

Masuno was repeating to her mother what she had told this morning. Her mother nodded at everything the girl said, and then she spoke, partly to the teacher, " They said boats had been wrecked, roofs had caved in, and that the walls of some houses had fallen down so that everybody could see through. I was so frightened I just had to come. But I'm so glad it was only a well-pole that broke."

After she had gone, Miss Oishi asked, " Mahchan, at whose house did the walls fall down ? "

Masuno looked proud again, almost forgetting to throw away the stone she was carrying, and replied, " It's at Nita's, Miss Oishi. Their walls fell, and their closets were wet all over. I went there to look. You could see the inside of their house from the street. Nita's grandma was looking up at the ceiling of the closet like this." With this, she frowned like his grandmother, which made Miss Oishi laugh.

" Closet ? Really ? " she said, while a fit of laughter welled up within her until at last it became so uncontrollable that she burst out laughing. The children did not know why she was laughing that way. Masuno alone looked glad, imagining that she was the one who had pleased her teacher. In the meantime, they had gotten near the general store. The proprietress, looking terribly angry, ran up and confronted Miss Oishi. The woman was so much out of breath that she could hardly speak at first. Immediately Miss Oishi stopped laughing and said, bowing, " Oh, excuse me. I'm sorry the storm was such a bad one. We're helping to clear away the stones today."

The proprietress, however, pretended not to hear anything and asked, " Lady Teacher, what were you laughing about just now? "

Miss Oishi said nothing.

" Is other people's bad luck so funny? My husband fell off the roof, but maybe that's funny too, is it? I'm sorry he didn't get hurt more. If he had, it would have been even funnier, huh? "

" I'm sorry. I didn't mean— "

" Never mind. Why did you laugh about others' bad luck then? Don't clean the road just for appearance's sake! Anyway, leave the street in front of my house as it is. . . . Huh—she's doing it just so she can ride her bicycle. Silly thing! She'd better do it by herself then." She muttered the last few sentences, as if talking to herself, and went away angrily, leaving the teacher speechless with surprise. The proprietress then talked to Carpenter Kawamoto's wife next door, purposely in a loud voice, " What a woman! Can you think of a teacher laughing at others' bad luck? I gave her a piece of my mind."

This, too, was certain to be exaggerated and spread all over the village in no time. Miss Oishi stood there for about two minutes, brooding over it. But, when she noticed the pupils surrounding her and looking worried, she smiled tearfully and managed to sound cheerful, saying, " Let's quit now. It was my own fault. Shall we sing songs on the beach? "

She turned around and led the children. The little ones were too observant not to notice a few tears falling from her eyes although she had a smile on her lips.

" She's crying."

" That old woman made her cry."

They whispered to each other a little and then became silent; only the sound of their sandals was heard. Miss Oishi thought of turning around to say, " I'm not crying," with a smile, but she felt the tears welling up again and kept silent. Perhaps she had been wrong in laughing on a day like this, she thought, but she had not been laughing about others' bad luck, as the proprietress had said. Rather, she had been laughing, first because Masuno's gesture had been so funny, and secondly because the word " closet " had reminded her of what Nita had said one day during the first term.

" Where's the emperor? " she had asked that day. Some pupils raised their hands. Nita was among them, for a change, and she called on him. With that loud voice of his, which sounded as if it were squeezed out of his whole body, he answered, " He's in the closet."

It was such an unexpected answer that the teacher laughed until tears came into her eyes. Not only she but all the children laughed, too. Their laughter made the classroom vibrate and reached far outside the school. Some pupils whispered " Tokyo " or " the Imperial Palace," but Nita did not seem to understand. When the laughter had calmed down, Miss Oishi asked him, " What do you mean by ' closet ' ? "

The boy spoke less self-confidently this time : " Isn't he hidden in the closet at school ? "

That explained it. He had meant the emperor's picture. Because the branch school had no shrine, the picture was kept locked up in the closet.

Miss Oishi had been reminded of this incident when she heard about the closet in Nita's house. Since the incident had taken place, the young Lady Teacher had been unable to suppress her laughter whenever she remembered it. But, of course, she could not have given such an explanation to the general store proprietress. She kept walking in silence. Even now, when she was crying, that incident seemed funny. But it was not funny enough to chase away the miserable feeling caused by the proprietress's words. Neither the teacher nor the pupils knew how to deal with their heavy hearts, except by singing songs on the beach. As soon as they got down to the beach, the teacher started singing, using her hands as a baton.

" *Early one spring, by a river, where reeds grow,*" she started singing " A Careless Barber." The children surrounded her and joined her.

> " *The crab opened a barber shop.*
> *Snip, snip, snip,*
> *Snip, snip, snip.*
> *The rabbit came in for a hair cut,*
> *Snip, snip, snip,*
> *Snip, snip, snip.*
> *The crab cut off the rabbit's ear.*
> *Snip, snip, snip,*
> *Snip, snip, snip.*"

While singing, they gradually began to feel cheerful.

> "*Angry, the rabbit ran away.*
> *Snip, snip, snip,*
> *Snip, snip, snip.*
> *The crab went off to his hole to hide.*"

Before the song was over, the teacher found herself laughing heartily again. She was pleased with the funny crab in the song, who had failed out of carelessness and had therefore something in common with her.

They sang all the songs they had learned during the first term, such as " This Road " and " A Plover." After singing " Boss on the Hill," they stopped for

a break and the children started running about. Only
five or six first graders remained quietly around the
teacher. The girls among them rarely groomed their
hair but tied it in a clumsy bun at the back of their
heads, and the boys' originally close-cropped hair
had grown so long that it almost covered their ears.
There was no barber shop in the village, so the hair
clipper at school proved very useful. It was Gentleman Teacher's job to give haircuts to the boys. As
for the girls with clumsy buns, Lady Teacher would
have to take care of them, by applying some mercurial
ointment to their scalps. Thinking of doing it tomorrow, she stood up and said, " This is all for today.
Let's go now."

She dusted her skirt at the knees, and stepped backward. Suddenly she screamed; she had fallen into
a sand trap. Some of the children screamed with
her; some approached laughing; some clapped their
hands for joy; some stood dumbfounded. Amid all
the clamor, the teacher did not try to get up. She
lay on her side, doubled up, with her hair touching
the sand. Those who had been laughing or clapping
their hands became silent. They all realized something had gone wrong. Seeing the tears falling from
the teacher's closed eyes, Sanae Yamaishi suddenly
cried out. Miss Oishi, as though she had been encouraged by the girl's cry, said, " I'm all right,"

and, with an effort, half sat up. She moved her leg in the pit gently and unbuttoned her shoe as cautiously as possible. The moment she touched her right ankle, however, she fell on her side again. She did not try to get up any more. After a while, she said, with her eyes shut, "Will one of you go and get Gentleman Teacher? Tell him I've got a broken leg and can't walk."

The children set up a great clamor. While the older ones rushed off to find Gentleman Teacher, the girls began crying loudly. As if they had heard a fire alarm, all the villagers dashed out of their houses and came running. Takeichi's father arrived first and approached Lady Teacher who lay with her head down. Kneeling down on the sand, he asked, "What's the matter, Miss Oishi?" and peered at her. But the teacher, whose face was distorted with pain, could not seem to say anything. The children told him that she had hurt her leg. He looked a little relieved then, and said, "You must have sprained your ankle. Let me see it." She gave a groan and grimaced even more. Her ankle had already swollen to almost twice its normal size. There was a clear mark on the skin where the shoe had been, but her ankle was not bleeding.

"We'd better put a cold compress on it," said Takeichi's father to the crowd of people who had gathered.

Kichiji Tokuda's father hastened away and returned with his soiled towel soaked with sea water.

Gentleman Teacher came up hurriedly and asked, " Does it hurt a lot? "

Lady Teacher merely nodded.

" Can't you walk? " he asked again. She shook her head.

" How about trying to get up anyway? "

Lady Teacher remained silent. Misako Nishiguchi's mother brought from her house a pad of cloth covered with a kind of ointment made from flour and egg.

" I don't think your bone's broken, but you'd better see a doctor or a masseur right away."

" Kusada in Naka-machi is the best masseur, I guess. He can set bones too."

" Dr. Hashimoto's better, I'm sure."

Various people made various suggestions. But anyway there was neither a surgeon nor a masseur in the cape village. However, one fact was clear: Miss Oishi could not possibly walk. After a great deal of wrangling, they finally decided to take her to Naka-machi by boat. Kotsuru Kabe's father and Takeichi's brother volunteered to row her in the boat belonging to Tadashi's father, a fisherman. Gentleman Teacher, who was going to acompany them, carried Lady Teacher on his back onto the boat. Each time she was picked up and laid down, she could not help groaning, no matter how much she tried to refrain from it.

As the boat was putting off from the beach, all the girls shouted at once with tears in their voices.

" Teacher ! "

" Lady Teacher ! " Some of them shouted at the top of their lungs. Miss Oishi could not move even a little. She kept silent, with her eyes shut, listening to their cries.

" Teacher ! "

While their voices became less and less audible, the boat moved far out into the bay. Across the bay, over which she had thrown a magic bridge only that morning, she now returned, bearing her pain.

3

Five Go* of Rice
and One *Sho* of Beans

Ten days passed. Half a month passed. Yet Lady
Teacher did not show up. Her bicycle, which stood
against the wall outside the faculty room, became
dusty. Sometimes the children were seen around the
bicycle, looking lonely. Some of them thought Miss
Oishi would never come back. Her absence was a
source of disappointment to the pupils going to the
main school, too. They had not realized until then
how much the teacher's bicycle had encouraged them
every day, and how much they had all looked forward
to meeting her on their long walks. The villagers
missed her, too. They regretted in their hearts that
they had not been very friendly to her, even though
none had been particularly mean to her. Suddenly
they began to speak well of Miss Oishi.

" We've never had a teacher like her. The children
took to her from the beginning."

"I hope she'll get better soon. I wouldn't want

* One *go* is one tenth of a *sho* and is about 0.16 quart.

her to be crippled by what our kids did. And besides, we'd have trouble getting a new teacher."

" I surely hope she'll be all right. It would be awful to be crippled at her age. How'd she get to school?"

And thus they talked about Lady Teacher. It was obvious that they really wanted her to return to the cape village. If she did not come back, they would be in real trouble. Gentleman Teacher was the one who suffered most right away. At the tiny village school, a music lesson was customarily given once a week. But even that one hour lesson was too much for him. During Lady Teacher's absence, at first, he let the children sing in unison what they had learned, and told the better ones to sing solo. In that way, about a month passed. But, because he could not temporize this way indefinitely, he finally decided to learn to play the organ. It certainly was a trying job. He would sing loudly, " 1-1-1-2-3-3-3-, 5-5-5-6-5 . . . ," instead of " Do - do - do - re- mi - mi - mi, sol-sol-sol-la-sol . . . ," because it was the way he had learned in primary school. " 3-3-3-3-2-2-2, 1-1-2-3-1 . . . ," he went on to sing.

The music lesson was scheduled for the third period on Saturday mornings. It had been so arranged because singing was supposed to make the pupils happy and put them into the right mood for the weekend.

But, all of a sudden, this lesson lost its attraction for the children as well as for the teacher. It was worse for Gentleman Teacher. As early as Thursday, he would begin to feel uneasy about the third period on Saturday. Becoming suddenly irritable, he would work off his bad temper on the pupils. He would scold a pupil just because he was looking away, or make another stand at the back of the room because he had forgotten to bring something.

"Doesn't Gentleman Teacher get angry often these days?"

"Isn't he mean? I wonder what's the matter."

While the children wondered what was the matter Gentleman Teacher's wife knew only too well. Inwardly she was worried, and she wanted to help her husband somehow. One Friday evening, stopping her part-time work of making straw plaits, she stood by the organ and encouraged him.

"I'll be your pupil, dear."

"Will you?"

The old couple by the organ looked so weird in the flickering light that they would have made a little girl's blood run cold. Gentleman Teacher and his wife went on singing in the semi-darkness: "1-1-1-2-3-3-3, 5-5-5-6-5 . . ."

The night was far advanced by the time the teacher had learned to play the organ to his wife's singing.

All the villagers had long since gone to sleep. As if she were afraid she might be disturbing them, she put out the small oil lamp, and, groping her way back to their room, she heaved a sigh and whispered to her husband: " Lady Teacher gives us a lot of trouble, doesn't she? "

" Yes, but she's got more trouble herself."

" That's true. Practicing the organ isn't so bad compared with a broken leg."

" Maybe Miss Oishi won't come back any more. She wasn't angry, but her mother was as angry as could be. She said, ' She's the only child I have. I'll never send her to your village again. People are so mean there.' "

" I don't blame her. But if Lady Teacher isn't coming back, we've got to have someone else."

Gentleman Teacher's wife whispered as if she did not like others to overhear, and sent a reproachful look across the bay. The Pine Tree village seemed peacefully asleep too, with a few lights flickering like stardust in the distance. It seemed to her that they must be the only two people who were staying up so late and working so hard. She felt resentful toward Lady Teacher.

Ever since the accident, Gentleman Teacher's wife had been helping at school, too, teaching sewing to the five fourth grade girls. This consisted principally

in quilting floorcloths, which were no trouble. All
she had to do during the class hour was to supervise,
while one girl after another sewed her floorcloth as
cautiously as if she were working figures on a thread
ball. But the music lessons were different, for playing
the organ was no easy job. It required much greater
skill than sewing. She was almost awe-stricken to see
her husband exerting all his energy to acquire this
skill. Although it was already October, Gentleman
Teacher perspired a great deal, practising the organ.
He sweat all the more, because the windows of the
classroom were kept closed so that no one could hear
him.

Being a teacher, he should have been able to play
the organ. But he had received only primary school
education and had become a teacher solely by self-
instruction, and so he was worse at playing the organ
than at anything else. Ordinarily country schools
had no special teachers for music, and every teacher
was supposed to be able to instruct his homeroom
pupils in music and gymnastics as well, but at the
cape school Lady Teacher customarily handled the
music instruction all by herself. That had been one
of the reasons why Gentleman Teacher had volunteered
to come to this isolated cape. Why then should he
struggle with the organ now? At times, he became
so angry that he could have smashed the organ.

But on this night it was different. He finally reached the stage where at last he was able to play accompaniment even if it was only for the singing of his wife. Gentleman Teacher felt pretty good and talked to her a little proudly: " I can learn to play the organ if I only try."

His wife nodded readily and said, " I know. I know."

The next day's music lesson was to be about the sixth since the beginning of Miss Oishi's absence. Gentleman Teacher almost looked forward to it.

" I'm sure the pupils will be surprised."

" So am I. They'll think better of you when they see you play the organ."

" That's right. They should be taught serious songs. Miss Oishi was just teaching them silly songs. She taught them ' A Plover ' and ' Snip, Snip, Snip,' all frivolous little songs like the ones they sing at a Bon Festival dance."

" The children like them, though."

" Do they? Those songs may be good for the girls, but they aren't the right kind of songs for the boys. It's about time I taught them the kind of song that arouses the Japanese spirit in them. After all, our pupils aren't all girls, you know."

He expanded his chest and, as if it were a matter of course, started singing to his wife the song they had just finished practicing.

"*Huge rocks are not so heavy—*"

His wife stopped him, saying, "Hush! If anybody heard you, he'd think you're crazy."

At last the next day came, and it was time for the music lesson. The pupils walked very slowly into the classroom. Their steps were heavy, probably because they thought that once again they would be made to sing without the accompaniment of the organ.

Miss Oishi used to remain in the classroom to play the organ after the second period on Saturday. When the thwacking board was struck to announce the beginning of the third period, she would play a march to pep up the pupils, and before they knew it, they would be marching into the classroom with light steps. How much fun it used to be, although they had not been quite conscious of it. But now that they no longer had Miss Oishi, there was a kind of dissatisfaction in their hearts that was equally unconscious.

"I'll listen. You just sing whatever you like," Gentleman Teacher would say, ignoring the organ. But the children had found it difficult to start singing without the accompaniment of the organ. Even when they did, they would often sing out of tune.

But it was a little different today. When they entered the room, Gentleman Teacher was already

seated in front of the organ. He did not press the
keys exactly in the same way as Lady Teacher, but he
did press a couple of them as a signal to make a bow.
There was an expression of wonder on the faces of
the pupils. As Lady Teacher had usually done, Gentleman Teacher had also written the music of the song
they were to learn on the right blackboard and its words
on the left one.

> " *Huge Rocks* "
> *Huge rocks are not so heavy*
> *As our duty toward our country.*
> *In war, we must go forward*
> *Through all the arrows and the bullets;*
> *We must rush forward*
> *To die for this our country.*

All the Chinese characters had phonetic symbols
next to them. Gentleman Teacher left the organ and
got up on the platform. Just as he did for other
subjects, he picked up a bamboo stick and began ex-
plaining the meaning of the song, pointing at each
word. It was just like a lesson in morals. He explained the profound meaning of the song over and
over again, but few really understood it. First the
first graders, then the second graders, became restless
and noisy. Some of the third and fourth graders
started talking in whispers. Then, all of a sudden,
there was a whacking noise. The teacher had brought

his stick down on his desk very hard. All at once, the pupils quieted down and looked at Gentleman Teacher with big, round eyes. The teacher spoke in a severe, yet somehow tender, tone: "It seems that Miss Oishi won't be coming to school for some time. So from now on I'll be your music teacher. I want you to remember the songs I'm going to teach you."

Then he went to the organ and sat there with his head down. He looked as though he were embarrassed. What was more remarkable, he started singing in that posture.

" 1-1-1-2-3-3-3, 5-5-5-6-5, all together!"

The pupils burst out laughing, for Gentleman Teacher sang solfa in the old-fashioned way. But, however much he was laughed at, he was unable to bring himself to sing in the modern way at his age. So finally he began with the scale and kept on teaching them in his own way. The children were quite pleased with the outcome.

" 3-3-3-3-2-2-2, 1-1-2-3-1, 2-2-2-2-1-3-5, 5-5-5-5-6-5-3. . . ."

They all sounded like crazy mathematicians. The pupils learned the funny way of singing the song in no time, and it became very popular with them from that day on. No one would sing the stirring and lively words of the song to please Gentleman Teacher. They would sing " 5-5-5-5-6-5-3 " instead.

On a Saturday, a few weeks later, the children were on their way home after singing the same old " Huge Rocks " at school. Masuno, a first grade girl, whispered in a precocious manner to Sanae, who was walking by her side : " I don't really care for Gentleman Teacher's music lessons at all. I prefer Lady Teacher's songs much more." Having said so, she started singing a song Lady Teacher had taught them.

" *A mountain crow brought me—* "

Sanae and Kotsuru joined in.

" *A small, red envelope.* "

Around them were only first grade girls, who had no classes in the afternoon.

" I wonder when Lady Teacher's coming back," said Masuno, looking at the Pine Tree. That led everybody else to look in the same direction.

" I'd like to see her," said Kotsuru.

Isokichi and Kichiji, catching up with them, joined in and repeated : " I'd like to see her." After they said so, they realized that they meant what they had just said. They stopped and looked at the Pine Tree together.

"Lady Teacher's in the hospital," Isokichi told them what he had heard. Kotsuru, however, disagreed : " She was in the hospital just at first. She's already out. Daddy told me he met her on the street yesterday."

That was probably why she had said, before anyone else, that she would like to see Lady Teacher. Her father, the "bellman," did all sorts of errands both by boat and on foot. He had pulled his cart into town the day before. He visited the towns surrounding the bay on other people's business at least every other day, and would come home with his boat or cart laden, and all sorts of gossip as well. The news about Miss Oishi—that she had had her Achilles' tendon broken, that she could not walk for another few months, and so on—had all been picked up by the bellman going his rounds, his bell swinging and clinging on his belt.

"Then, do you think she'll come pretty soon? I hope she will," said Sanae, her eyes sparkling with anticipation. Kotsuru contradicted her again: "How could she? She can't even stand up yet." She then went on to suggest, "How about all of us going to Lady Teacher's house?" and looked around at one face after another. By that time Takeichi, Tadashi, and Nita had joined them. None of the children, however, agreed to Kotsuru's idea right away. They just looked at the Pine Tree silently, for they had no idea how far it would be. They had heard it was five miles one way, or two *ri*, as grown-ups would put it. But, being inexperienced in walking, the first graders could not imagine very well how long the distance would really be. It might be an awfully

long way, yet the Pine Tree seemed to stand right
across the bay.   There was one thing that worried
them a little : the fact that Lady Teacher's village was
farther than Ujigami Shrine.   They had never walked
as far as the Pine Tree.   They had gone part of the
way several times, to visit the shrine at the time of
the annual festival, either on foot or by boat.   No
one knew, however, how long the rest of the distance
would be.   Only Nita had been to the town beyond
the Pine Tree just recently.   But, on that trip, he had
merely taken a bus from the shrine and had passed by
the Pine Tree.   Nevertheless, all the children surrounded him.

" Nita, how many hours did it take from the shrine
to the Pine Tree ? "

Nita answered proudly, ignoring his runny nose.
" It took only a little time.   The bus blew its horn
when it whizzed by the Pine Tree.   I didn't even finish
eating a bun."

" You liar !   It takes only a minute to eat a bun,"
yelled Takeichi.

Matsue turned to Misako for support.   " I know
buses run very fast, but one minute doesn't sound
right, does it ? "

Nita was irritated by their opposition and said,
" But I began eating a bun when I got into the bus
in front of the shrine, and I still had it in my hand

when I got off."

"Are you sure?"

"Sure!"

"Will you swear?"

"Of course, I will."

At last they all believed him. The fact was, however, that Nita had been so excited on his first bus
trip that he had been watching the way the driver
had handled the bus, forgetting all about the bun.
But no one thought of that. They just figured out
that the distance between the shrine and the Pine
Tree must be fairly short, because Nita, the only one
who had taken a bus, said he had not had time enough
to finish a bun before he had reached the next town
beyond the Pine Tree. It was true that Lady Teacher
had used a bicycle to come from the Pine Tree village,
but hadn't she arrived at school so early every
morning? To the children, this seemed to make the
distance appear to be short rather than the contrary.
Then a decisive factor was added: they saw a bus
running along the road by the sea just across the
bay. The bus looked as small as a speck and disappeared into a wood in no time.

"Oh, I want to go!" exclaimed Masuno in that
voice of hers which, strangely enough, influenced even
boys.

Tadashi and Takeichi agreed.

" Let's go ! "

" Okay.   Let's ! "

Kotsuru and Matsue jumped for joy and excitement.

" Let's go.   Let's run over and run back."

" That's it.   That's it."

Only Sanae and Kotoe remained silent.   Sanae did not say anything because she was born quiet.   Kotoe, on the other hand, looked confused.   She must have been thinking of her home.

" Aren't you coming, Kotoe ? " asked Kotsuru as if accusing her.   Kotoe looked even more uneasy and replied, " I'll ask Grandma first."

Her faint voice did not sound confident.   Although Kotoe was only a first grader, she had four younger brothers and sisters, and because she was the oldest child, she always had a baby strapped to her back. She had been baby-tending since the age of three or so.   If she went home and talked to her family, she would never be allowed to go.   The same thing would happen to Sanae, Matsue, and Kotsuru.   For a while, they looked at one another in discouragement.   There had been an unwritten understanding since long ago that the village children might spend their time in play up to their eighth or ninth year.   But even while they played, they were not entirely free to do as they wanted.   They always had to have either their little brothers or sisters around them or babies on their

backs. The only children who could play in any way
they liked were Masuno and Misako, because they
had no brothers nor sisters.

Kotoe's answer had reminded the children of all
this, but they did not feel like giving up their plan.

" Let's all sneak out of our houses after lunch,"
Kotsuru urged the others, as though there were no
turning back.

" That's it ! If we tell our families, they may not
let us go. Let's not say anything. Let's just go."
Takeichi, the bright boy, made the decision. No one
disagreed any more. The secrecy of the whole plan
excited them all the more.

" Let's all sneak out and meet above the wharf,"
suggested Tadashi.

Masuno, the leader, thought even more carefully
and said, " The wharf's too close to the general
store. We don't want the old woman to see us.
Let's meet near the grove."

" That's a good idea. Let's take the road between
the fields."

Each of them suddenly became busy.

" We must run all the way over and back, do you
understand ? " Kotoe made sure of it again. After
they went off, Kotoe walked on, thinking very hard.
But try as she might, she could think of no way of
sneaking out. Should she give up? No, she couldn't.

If she did, no one would play with her from tomorrow on. She didn't want to be left out. Yet she didn't want to be scolded later by Grandma or Mummy even if she could sneak out of her house.

" I wish we didn't have a baby at home," she thought. She usually loved her baby brother Takeshi, but this time she remembered him with a sudden hatred, and she wanted a holiday away from him. She suddenly turned around and made for the fields. When the grove came into sight, she started running. Her heart beat fast for fear that someone might be watching her.

Two hours passed, and Kotoe's Grandma was the first to feel anxious. " She must be hungry. I wonder what's keeping her," she muttered to herself, at first. She intented to strap Takeshi to Kotoe's back, if she came home, and then go to the fields to do the second picking of cowpeas. But the girl was not back yet. It would do no good to go fetch her at the school because Kotoe could not possibly be there any more. She picked up the baby and the sash to strap him on with, and went to the house of Kotoe's best friend, Sanae, to look there, thinking that the child would certainly be playing with Sanae and that she had forgotten all about the time of day.

" Hello ! Is Koto around? " she asked.

Of course, the girl was not there. Not only that, Sanae was not back, either. The old woman looked about the grounds of Kojin Shrine on her way home, but the children there, playing under the cedars, were either a little older or a little younger, and not Kotoe or her friends. She asked the children loudly, " Did you see my granddaughter Koto? "

" No."

" I haven't seen her today."

" Isn't she at Sanae's? "

The children gave her one reply after another, but offered no encouragement.

" Good-for-nothing girl! If you see her, tell her I want her to come home right away, will you? "

She flung the baby up on her back and talked to him as though expecting him to understand her: " Where's your sister anyway? We'll have to give her a good scolding when she comes back."

But she was getting a little anxious, remembering that the girl had not even had her lunch yet. While she was in her house making straw sandals on the dirt floor and worrying, Carpenter Kawamoto's wife came hurring up as if she were worried about something, too.

" Hello! Fine day, isn't it? I came for Matsu, but I don't see her."

At this, Kotoe's Grandma stopped her sandal-making

for a moment and said, " Can't you find Matchan, either? I wonder where the kids could be loafing. They haven't even had lunch."

" Matsu came home for lunch all right. But after lunch she went out as if she had something to do. I thought she'd be back soon, but she isn't back yet."

Suddenly Kotoe's Grandma felt very uneasy. She could no longer work on sandals. After the carpenter's wife left to look for Matsue elsewhere, the old woman became more anxious, now going out, now coming in; now standing, now sitting. She could not keep still.

" I don't blame her. Kids of her age want to play a lot, and yet she has to do baby-sitting every day. It's only natural for her to feel like rebelling."

A tear dropped. Before her eyes, dim with tears, floated the figure of little Kotoe and would not disappear. The poor girl was sway-backed, probably from having carried babies on her back too much since infancy.

" But where in the world is she anyway? And what's she doing? And her parents are pretty late today too."

She went outdoors and gazed out across the sea. It seemed to her that Kotoe's parents, fishing for horse mackerel, were also unusually late in coming back today.

By the time the carpenter's wife came over to ask "Isn't Kotoe back yet?" for the third time, Kotsuru's sister, Sanae's brother, and Fujiko's mother had come to inquire for their sisters or daughters. They soon found out that all the first graders were missing. A little later, they learned that one of the older pupils had seen the children near the Hachimando Stationery Store while on his way back from the main school, and they were now only half as anxious. In the meantime, rumors spread all over the village, and people said whatever they felt like.

"I hear there's some kind of show in town. They must have gone to see it."

"How could they? They didn't have any money."

"Maybe they're just looking at the posters and signs with their mouths open."

"Aren't kids curious!"

The parents of the first grade children talked to one another, too. They were half smiling now.

"They'll come back pretty soon, as hungry as wolves and with lots of blisters on their feet, I bet."

"I wonder what they'll look like when they come back, the idiots!"

"I don't know whether to scold my child or not."

"But we can't praise them, can we?"

They sounded optimistic now because, to their relief, Isokichi's brother, Nita's father, and Fujiko's father had gone to meet the children. Still, how careless of them that none of them thought of Miss Oishi!

In the meantime, the three who were on their way to get the children reached the principal village. Each time they came across someone who might have seen the children, they would ask: " Excuse me, but did you see about ten little kids passing by early this afternoon? About six or seven years old? "

Many times they repeated the same question, but with little success.

What were the children doing all that while?

Needless to say, it was Kotoe who got to the grove first. There she hid her school bag in the grass and waited for the others. Kichiji and Isokichi came running, as if racing each other. Then came Take-ichi and Tadashi. Fujiko and Nita were the last to arrive. Nita was foresighted enough to have all four pockets of his shirt and trousers filled up with parched broad beans. He said he had brought all the parched beans he could lay his hands on. He distributed some to each of his friends, looking happier than all the others. They set out, munching the beans.

" Lady Teacher'll be surprised."

" Gee, she'll be glad, won't she? "

Kotoe walked alone at the head of the group and

looked back at the others. For people who were supposed to be running there and back, she thought, they were walking awfully slowly. The children talked about nothing but Lady Teacher although they were sure to find out all about her once they got there.

"Lady Teacher limps."

"I wonder if her foot still hurts."

"She wouldn't limp if it didn't."

Then Isokichi took a few quick steps forward and said, "Look! This is the Achilles' tendon. This thick tendon broke, see?"

He rubbed around his own Achilles' tendon and added: "It broke right here. It must hurt a lot."

At last the children's pace became quicker. It was the first time they had ever taken this road all by themselves. Every time they rounded a turn, there was a change of scenery, so they never tired of going on. As the road crossed the cape and ran along the bay side, the Pine Tree village became more distant, obliquely behind their backs. They began to feel uncertain as to whether they were actually heading in the right direction, but no one would say anything about it. After a while, they saw in the distance the group of older pupils coming home from the main school. They looked at one another in alarm.

"Hide! Hide! Hurry up!" Masuno's call made

the other eleven run into a thicket of pampas grass near by as nimbly as monkeys. The grass rustled violently.

"Keep still! Don't make any noise!" said Masuno, curling her thin lips and glaring at the others with her long, slanted eyes. Even Takeichi and Tadashi became quiet and motionless. The thicket of pampas grass, almost twice as tall as the children, rustled a little with all twelve of them in it. It was entirely owing to Masuno's quick wits, however, that they were not noticed by the older ones passing by. Masuno could make all her classmates as gentle as kittens by glaring at them.

By the time they came to the end of the cape path and entered the principal village, they were talking much less loudly. There were many towns and villages of various sizes on the way to the Pine Tree village. The children entered and passed through them one after another until at last they got tired of the repetition, yet they could never seem to reach the Pine Tree. From the cape village, the tree had seemed so near; it had been right before them. The same tree, however, was not even in sight now. The children's feet began to make them realize how long five miles, or two *ri* by adults, really was, and they became more and more quiet. The people they met were all strangers. They felt as though they had come to a far-away land, and gradually their loneliness began to weigh them down like a heavy stone.

None of them realized that one more bend would bring the Pine Tree fully into their view, but they did realize that Nita's memory was far from reliable, and had given up bothering him with questions. They could only keep on and on going step after step. Takeichi and Misako were the first to wear out their straw sandals. Takeichi gave Misako one of his sandals which was still wearable, and walked on barefoot. Kichiji's and Tadashi's sandals were about to wear out, too. But no one had a penny, so they could not possibly buy new ones. Those whose sandals were wearing out felt more miserable than the others, being aware that they might have to go home barefoot back along that interminable road.

All of a sudden, Kotoe began crying. It was probably because she had not had any lunch that she had tired more quickly than the others and could not stand it any longer. She crouched by the road-side and cried loudly. That caused Misako and Fujiko to sob, too. The other children stopped and looked at the crying girls absently. They felt like crying themselves and could say nothing to cheer up the girls. Now was the time to turn back. Now was the time for someone to suggest " Let's go home! " Yet no one could bring himself to say even that much.

Even Masuno and Kotsuru looked embarrassed. In
fact, they felt like crying, too. But they refrained.
If all of them had cried, someone might have come to
help them, but they did not think of that.

The early autumn sky was perfectly clear; the afternoon sun beat down from behind on this dejected
group of little children standing in the emptiness of
the white, dry dirt road. They felt so homesick
that unconsciously they stood facing the direction
they had come from. From that way came a silver-
colored bus, sounding its horn. Instantly the twelve
children, of one accord, stood back to let the bus pass,
lining up in the grass by the side of the narrow road.
Even Kotoe stopped crying and gazed intently at the
bus. As the bus passed by the children, raising clouds
of white dust, an unexpected face appeared in the
window. No sooner had she exclaimed " Oh, my! "
than the bus had passed by. It was Miss Oishi.

" Hurrah ! " Without thinking, the children jumped
back onto the road and ran after the bus, shouting
for joy. They ran fast as though their feet were imbued
with new strength.

" Teacher ! "

" Lady Teacher ! "

The bus stopped, let Lady Teacher off, and started
again. The teacher waited for the children, leaning
on her crutches. Without waiting for them to come

near, she shouted, " What in the world is the matter? "

The children longed to run up to her and cling to her arms, yet they knew they should not. Partly from too much affection, partly from shyness, some stood still without coming up close to her.

" We came to see you. It was awfully far." Nita spoke first, whereupon all the others began to talk.

" We promised not to tell our parents before we came."

" We couldn't see the Pine Tree for so long Kotoe began to cry."

" Miss Oichi, where's the Pine Tree? Is it still far? "

" Does your foot still hurt? "

Although the teacher was smiling, tears streamed down her cheeks. When she told the children that her house in the Pine Tree village was just around the bend, they shouted with joy.

" But it seemed like a long way! "

" We almost gave up and turned back, didn't we? "

With the teacher on crutches in the middle, they all walked to her house. Her mother was completely taken by surprise, and suddenly became busy—lighting the cooking stove, and running out of the house many times on errands. The children stayed there about an hour. While they were there, they were treated to noodles with fried bean curd, and some even had seconds. The teacher was very glad and suggested they have a souvenir picture taken. She asked the photographer in the neighborhood and took the children to the Pine Tree.

" I'd like to have you with me longer," she said, " but it's going to be dark pretty soon. Your parents must be worrying about you."

The children did not want to go home, but Miss Oishi talked them into it and finally put them all on a boat. It was past four o'clock. Days being short in fall, the sun was already going down in the west. The dusk was gathering over the cape village as though nothing special had occurred there that day.

" Good-by ! "

" Good-by ! "

From the boat came shouts of farewell to the teacher, who gazed after them from the beach, leaning on her crutches.

While the three men searched all the towns and villages, the twelve children arrived back at their village from an unexpected direction.

" Hi ! "

" Hello ! "

The sudden cries from the sea took the cape villagers by surprise. At first, the parents scolded their children, but at last they all burst out laughing, and thought better of Miss Oishi.

Two days later, strange packages were put on the bellman's cart. They were so small that he had to put them all in an empty apple box before pulling the cart out of the village. After doing all sorts of errands on his way, he reached the Pine Tree. Shouldering the box just the way it was, he carried it along, the bell on his belt ringing at each step he took. With a final tinkle, it stopped ringing at the porch of Miss Oishi's house. The bellman's bell always signified presents sent from somewhere, and further explanation was usually unnecessary.

" There! Five *go* of rice and one *sho* of beans. This one's pretty light. Maybe it's dried fish. Another five *go* of rice and one *sho* of beans ! . . . "

He took out one small bag after another and heaped them all on the porch. There were names on the bags. These were all get-well presents of rice and beans from the grateful villagers.

4

Parting

In the finished picture, the teacher was leaning on her crutches with the Pine Tree in the background, surrounded by the twelve children, some standing and the others squatting. Miss Oishi looked at each one in turn—Isokichi, Takeichi, Matsue, Misako. . . . When she came to Nita, she found him in such a strained position that she burst out laughing. He looked very stiff as though he would explode unless he let out his breath. His position of " attention " would have made anyone laugh. It was the first picture the pupils had ever had taken, except Masuno and Misako, and that was why most of them looked so tense. Nita and Kichiji were the worst of all. Contrary to Nita, Kichiji was shrinking from the camera, with his face turned away and his eyes closed. The way he looked was so typical of his usual shy self that Miss Oishi felt sorry for him.

" Poor Kitchin ! He must have been scared. Maybe he was afraid something would jump out at him from the camera."

While she was looking at the picture, smiling to

herself, the principal of the main school came for a visit. His voice made her stiffen like Nita in the picture. She went to the front door. Although no longer using crutches, she was still limping quite a bit. The principal watched her walk with a sympathetic frown.

" What an awful time you've had ! "

" I'm much better now, though."

" Does it still hurt? "

While she was wondering what to answer, her mother replied for her, thinking that the principal had come to urge her to go back to school.

" I'm very sorry Hisako's causing you so much trouble for so long. She seems to be much better now, but she isn't well enough to ride her bicycle yet. That's why she's still staying home, you know."

But the principal had not come with the intention of pressing her. He had merely come to inquire after Miss Oishi's health and to tell her good news. He called his friend's daughter by her first name today, as he talked to her: " Hisako, you've already sacrificed one of your feet, so I think you'd better quit the branch school now. I've made up my mind to have you teach at the main school, but from the way you walk, I'm afraid you can't teach there yet."

Miss Oishi's mother's eyes suddenly filled with

tears. She said, " Oh, my ! " but was unable to add anything more. The news was such a pleasant surprise that she could not think of the right words of thanks immediately. Noticing that her daughter had been remaining silent for some time, and in order to cover up her own embarrassment, she urged her.

" Hisako, where's your tongue? Why don't you thank him? "

But Miss Oishi was not very happy about this well-meant arrangement of the principal's. Half a year before, she would have jumped for joy, but for some reason she could not react so simply any more. What came out of her mouth, therefore, were not words of thanks.

" Er-r-r. . . . Is it already settled? Have you already appointed a teacher to take my place? "

" Yes, it was settled at the faculty meeting yesterday. Do you have any objection? "

" Of course I haven't any right to object. But I really don't know what to do."

Her mother might have scolded her if she had been there, but she had gone out, to buy cakes or something.

" What's the matter? " asked the principal with a big smile.

" Well, I promised my pupils to go back to them."

" For Heaven's sake ! How do you expect to get

there every day though? Your mother told me you couldn't ride your bicycle for some time. That's why I made this arrangement."

There was no other excuse she could make, and yet she longed all the more to return to the cape village. Still feeling reluctant to give up, she could not help asking, " Who's taking my place? "

" Mrs. Goto."

" Oh ! "

She almost said " Isn't that a shame? " but refrained at the last minute. This time she was anxious about Mrs. Goto, not about herself, wondering how the new teacher would get to school every day. Mrs. Goto was nearly forty years old, and had a nursing baby besides, for she had married late. True, she lived a little closer to the cape, and yet how would she get to school every day, a distance of four miles, with the cold months approaching? Miss Oishi suddenly looked up and spoke half out of sympathy for her, half out of her own reluctance to give up.

" Sir, how about this? As soon as my foot gets completely well, I'll take Mrs. Goto's place. Can she substitute for me just until then? "

She thought it was a very good idea, but the principal's answer surprised her.

" Aren't you conscientious, Hisako! You don't have to be so thoughtful. Everything worked out very well, because Mrs. Goto herself wished to go to the cape."

" Why was that? "

" We were going to ask her to retire next year because of old age, but if she went to the cape, she'd be able to teach about three more years. When I told her so, she accepted the offer gladly."

" Old age? Goodness! "

" Old age " at thirty-seven or eight? Did they call a woman with a nursing baby old? Rather astonished, Miss Oishi said no more. Her mother, who had come home by that time and was passing around a tray with fruit and things on it, was quite embarrassed at her daughter's bluntness.

" What a way to talk, Hisako! You haven't even thanked him enough for his kindness. I've been letting you do the talking, but you've been saying nothing but peculiar things ever since he came."

She bowed to the principal and said, " I'm afraid I haven't brought Hisako up right. Since she's my only child, I guess I've been too easy on her without realizing it. That's how she picked up such an impolite way of talking. Yet she seems to be thinking of nothing but her school day and night. She's been very anxious to go back there. Now that you've been kind enough to transfer her to the main school, I'm sure she can start going to school by bus in about ten days. As you see, she's awfully stubborn, but won't you put up with her for my sake?"

She said all the things she would have liked her daughter to say, and bowed low several times. She winked at her daughter hintingly, but Miss Oishi ignored her and still kept on talking about Mrs. Goto.

"And is Mrs. Goto already teaching there?"

It seemed to amuse the principal to deal with this somewhat eccentric, perverse girl.

"Not yet. We can have another faculty meeting and cancel the whole thing if that's what you want. I'm afraid Mrs. Goto will be disappointed, though."

Miss Oishi's mother alone continued to feel anxious and nervous. The principal spoke to her, "Hisako reminds me of her father. She's as stubborn as he was. You know, he went on strike when he was only in primary school, which is unheard-of."

He laughed loudly. Miss Oishi had heard that story before. She remembered that her father, when a fourth grader, had been infuriated when his homeroom teacher had misunderstood him, and had incited his classmates to go on strike for a day. His classmates, including the present principal, all sympathized with him, marched into the village office together, and asked for a new teacher. This last spring, when Miss Oishi and her mother had visited the principal to ask him to get her a position, they had been told about this incident of her father's childhood for the first time and had laughed together. The principal was laughing again now, amused at the pleasant memories the story brought back. Strangely, however, the same story made Miss Oishi turn serious today.

After the principal left, Miss Oishi remained sunk in deep thought. Her mother spoke to her, trying to comfort her: " Things turned out pretty well after all, didn't they, Hisako? " But Miss Oishi kept silent.

At the supper table, she did not eat as much as usual. She kept thinking until late at night and finally spoke to her mother: " Maybe so—both for me and for Mrs. Goto." It was four hours after her mother had said, " Things turned out pretty well after all, didn't they, Hisako? "

Her mother agreed, looking relieved. " Yes, yes. I must say everything worked out very well, Hisako."

Again, Miss Oishi thought for a while and said in a determined manner: " I disagree completely. Not everything worked out very well—at least, not for Mrs. Goto. Why, it's rude to call her old."

Her mother did not try to object any more, but spoke gently as if her daughter needed to be calmed: " Let's go to bed anyway. It's pretty late now."

The next morning, Miss Oishi made up her mind to visit the cape village by boat. The ferryman was the bellman of the Pine Tree village whose occupation was, like that of Kotsuru's father, to ferry people and drag carts. It was a windless morning in late October. Both the sky and the sea were perfectly blue, and the refreshing sea air was so chilly that Miss Oishi instinctively hugged herself, using her kimono sleeves to keep warm.

"How cold! It'll soon be time for lined kimonos, won't it, Uncle?"

"No, it's not really that cold when the sun comes up. This is the best time of year. It's neither hot nor cold."

Miss Oishi, for a change, had on a serge kimono with small white checks, and an over-skirt of bluish purple. A mat was spread on the bottom of the boat, and she was sitting on it with her legs out sideways. Fortunately, however, her skirt hid her awkward posture. Across the deep, blue sea went the boat straight on, the teacher intent on the cape and the scull making regular sounds. In high spirit, she was now crossing the bay, over which she had come crying two months before.

"You really had a tough time, didn't you?"

"Yes."

"Young people have such soft bones they mend quickly when they break."

"It was neither a bone nor a muscle. It was what

they call the Achilles' tendon and it doesn't mend as readily as a bone does."

"Really? That was even worse then."

"But the kids didn't mean to do any harm. It was just an accident, so I can't complain."

"Even though—they gave you—such a hard time, —you're going—to say—good-by—to them.—Aren't you—good-natured! Heave ho!" The ferryman said this in short sentences to match the rythmn of his oar, and as he said "Heave ho!" he rowed even harder. Miss Oishi, giggling, spoke in the same way.

"You say so,—but those kids,—imagine,—they are only—in the first grade,—came to see me—without a word—to their parents.—How can I quit—until I've seen them?—Heave ho!"

Her merry laughter put the ferryman in a good mood. He said, "We mustn't forget—courtesy—and loincloths.—That's the way—life is.—Heave ho!"

At last Miss Oishi laughed to her heart's content, her sides shaking. On the sea, there was no fear of disturbing anyone. Her laughter, too, was punctuated with the sounds of the scull, as the boat advanced farther and farther out until it finally approached the village across the bay. Although the tip of the cape was still partly covered with the smoke from the cooking stoves, the day's work seemed to have long since started, and innumerable little sounds were heard.

"What are all the children doing about this time?" the teacher wondered. "Matsue, who used to rush out when I got to the general store on my bike; Iso-kichi, who used to wait for me above the wharf; Nita, who was late for school about once a week; Kichiji, who wet his pants in class twice during the first term. . . ." As she reminisced about one child after another, Miss Oishi marvelled again at their courage in coming all the way to the Pine Tree village at such a young age. Picturing those little, dusty feet on that day, she trembled with love and longing.

"Last time I was the one who was taken by surprise, so today I'll surprise them in return. I wonder who'll notice me first." While the teacher was thus occupied in happy expectation, the boat advanced farther and farther, and the cape, with its green woods and small black roofs, seemed to slide toward her. Two little girls were standing on the beach, looking in her direction. They did not look like first graders, and had their eyes fixed on the boat curiously. The vil-lagers on the cape, where life was monotonous, were quick to catch sight of outsiders coming either by sea or by land, and a group of curious people would gather in no time. This time, too, the number of children standing there increased to five, seven. . . . Finally the boat got close enough so that their clamor became audible, and their faces were distinguishable.

However, none of the children seemed able to make out who the kimono-clad woman was. They all watched her with serious faces. Even when she smiled at them, they still did not seem to know who it was. She became impatient, and before she knew it, had raised her hand to wave. The clamor suddenly became louder, and the children started shouting.

" That's Lady Teacher after all."

" Lady Teacher ! "

" Lady Teacher's here ! "

By that time some grown-ups had joined the children to give the teacher a hearty welcome. The rope the ferryman threw to shore was pulled so hard with shouts of joy that the boat was hauled up on the beach. After remaining on the beach laughing and talking for a while, Miss Oishi and the children started for the school. The poeple she met on her way all spoke to her and inquired after her health : " How's your foot ? I was worried about you."

The teacher answered each one of them in turn, " I'm much better, thank you. It was very kind of you to send me a present of rice the other day."

" Not at all. It was only a little present."

After a while, she met a man with a hoe on his shoulder. He was about to pull off his hand towel from around his head. He expressed his sympathy in about the same way as the others. Miss Oishi said,

" Thank you very much for the beautiful broad beans you gave me the other day."

The man smiled a little. " Oh, we gave you sesame seeds."

The teacher realized the foolishness of trying to be specific and decided not to mention either rice or beans any more. Because she had taught there for only a term, it was difficult for her to identify the villagers other than the parents of the first graders. The next man she met looked like a fisherman. He seemed to be the one who had given her some fish, so she made a bow and spoke to him cautiously.

" Thank you very much for the nice get-well present you gave me the other day."

The man suddenly looked embarrassed. " Er. . . . I meant to send you a present, but somehow or other, it got too late, and I didn't."

The teacher, too, was embarrassed and blushed. " Oh, I'm terribly sorry. It was my mistake."

Before the accident, they would have said that Lady Teacher had hinted for a get-well present. After she went past the man, the children burst out laughing. One of the boys said, " Miss Oishi, Seiichi's father has never given anybody anything. He just receives. You see, even when he feels like urinating, working in the woods, he'll walk a long way to his own fields just to do it."

The children all laughed. Miss Oishi had heard that story once before. The man's son, a fourth grader, had been the only one who would not bring a music notebook. One day, she had asked him why, wondering if he had forgotten to bring his notebook every time. He had looked down as if he were going to cry. Then the boy sitting next to him had answered for him, " His father says music doesn't teach him how to make money, and he won't buy him a notebook."

At the next music lesson, she had given the little boy, Seiichi, a notebook. She remembered now how gladly he had received it. All the textbooks he had were used ones. Yet his father was known as the second richest man in the village.

Miss Oishi was relieved that Seiichi was not there. Just then Nita asked her, " Does your foot still hurt? " He was the first to ask her a question. Although the teacher was no longer using crutches, she was still limping, and Nita must have felt sorry about it.

" Can't you ride your bicycle yet? " asked Kotsuru next.

" Well, maybe I'll be able to in half a year or so."

" Are you coming to school by boat then? " At Isokichi's question, the teacher merely shook her head. Kotoe was surprised and asked: " Oh, really? Are you coming on foot then? Can you walk such a long way? "

For Kotoe, the five-mile road must have been un-forgettable. She had been the first to begin crying because she had been hungry and anxious. On that day, she had hidden her school bag in a bush and gone, simply because she had not wanted to be left out. When the children were sent home by boat, she was depressed unlike everyone else. She was nervous, afraid of how much she would be scolded. But Grand-ma, who had come out to meet her, was more im-patient than any of the other parents; she walked into the water without waiting for a plank to be put across, and picked Kotoe out of the boat before any of the other children. While the other children walked down the plank to their parents as trium-phantly as victorious generals, only Kotoe and her Grandma cried. After they had gone around to the bush and picked up the bag, they made for home. By that time, they were both talking normally together.

" Don't go anywhere from now on without letting me know. Tell me before you go."

" But you always say No when I ask you."

" Yes, that's true. I must say you're right." Her Grandma gave a weak, tremulous laugh. " But any-way you must eat your lunch before you go. It's bad for you not to."

Grandma's remark reminded Kotoe of the noodles

she had had at Miss Oishi's. They had tasted so
good that the mere memory of them made her mouth
water. Her hunger of that day had made them taste
many times better than normal and imprinted their
taste on her palate.

Ever since then, every time the girl thought of the
noodles, she thought of Miss Oishi, or vice versa.
Now that Miss Oishi had come back unexpectedly,
Kotoe had asked " Can you walk such a long way? "
thinking of that long road and the noodles again.
However, it was not only Kotoe but all the children
who thought the teacher would teach at school again
from today on. No one seemed to be in doubt about
it, which made the teacher realize that she should have
announced why she had come today the minute she
had landed.

She reflected with regret that if she had gotten off
the boat, shouting " I came to say good-by," it would
have created a desirable atomosphere right away.
Making the best use of Kotoe's question, she spoke
slowly.

" It's a long way, isn't it? If I came all the way,
limping like this, it would be dark before I got here.
So it's . . . you see . . . no good."

Yet the children could not guess what she meant.
Tadashi, the fisherman's son, made a suggestion
which was quite like him.

" Miss Oishi, why don't you come by boat then? I'll pick you up every day. The Pine Tree village is no distance."

He had learned lately how to scull and was quite proud of it. The teacher could not help smiling. " Will you really? And will you give me a ride home in the afternoon? "

" Sure. Won't we? " Tadashi asked Isokichi. Perhaps he felt a little less confident now and needed his friend's assurance. Isokichi nodded.

" Thank you. I wish I had known it earlier. But the trouble is I have quit school already."

The children said nothing.

" So I came to say good-by today."

They still remained silent.

" Another Lady Teacher's coming pretty soon. Will you all be good pupils? I love it here very much, but I can't beat this foot. I'll come back when I get well."

They all looked down at the teacher's feet. Sanae's eyes filled with tears ; she kept them wide open to keep the glistening tears from overflowing. The moment Miss Oishi saw Sanae's tears,—Sanae, who usually did not express her feelings in words,—her own eyes, too, swelled with tears. Then, Masuno burst out crying as if she had touched a bee hive or something. That caused Kotoe, Misako, and even the strong-willed Kotsuru to sob. There was a chorus of crying and sobbing.

On both sides of the stone gate, where the sign board of the branch school was hung, stood a tall willow tree and a tall pine tree. Under the willow tree, surrounded by about thirty-five pupils, Lady Teacher no longer tried to suppress her tears. With Masuno leading the chorus so loudly, even Kichiji and Nita almost cried, but they seemed to be trying not to. Some of the older pupils stood by amusedly. Gentleman Teacher saw the scene from the window of the faculty room, slipped into his slippers made out of the tips of old shoes, and came running. When he heard the story, he said, "What's the matter with all of you? It was very kind of Lady Teacher to come today, wasn't it? You must welcome her with smiles. Why do you all cry so loudly? Get out of my way now. Lady Teacher, please come right in."

Yet they remained where they were, and went on sobbing.

"I give up. They say women and children are hard to deal with. I'll let you cry until you're satisfied. Cry as much as you want to."

When Gentleman Teacher pattered back in his slippers, they began laughing at last: they had found it funny to be told to cry.

The thwacking-board announced the beginning of

school, and the day's work was getting on its way. Miss Oishi had meant to leave after making a farewell speech at the morning assembly. When she had made her farewells, however, she stepped into the classroom of the first and second graders, as if urged on by something. The children all felt exuberant, having Lady Teacher with them again after such a long absence.

" Let's spend this one period together and then say good-by. This is actually an arithmetic class, but we can do something else if you want to. What'll we do? "

Lots of hands were raised, with shouts of " Call on me! " Before the teacher called upon anyone, Masuno shouted " Singing! " There were cries of joy and clapping of hands. They all seemed to approve of the idea.

Masuno suggested again: " Let's sing on the beach."

They gave another shout of joy.

" Miss Oishi, let's sing on the beach." Masuno kept on being the leader.

" Will you tell Gentleman Teacher and see me to the beach then? The boat is waiting for me there."

The children clapped their hands and rattled their desks. They talked to Gentleman Teacher about it, and he suggested everyone see Lady Teacher off.

They started with the limping Miss Oishi in the middle and the twelve first graders leading the procession. Gentleman Teacher walked at the rear, pushing Lady Teacher's bicycle, which had been accumulating dust since the day of the accident. The villagers they met on their way followed them to the beach.

"Don't cry this time," said Miss Oishi, peering at the faces of the children in turn. "Now cross your heart and promise me not to cry, Mahchan."

"All right."

"You also, Kotoe."

"All right."

"And you, Sanae."

"All right."

Those three were the worst crybabies. Now that they had given her their word, it would be all right, thought Miss Oishi.

While the girls were crossing their hearts, the whole group arrived at the beach. Looking at Masuno, Nita asked loudly: "What are we going to sing?"

"'Auld Lang Syne,' of course," answered Gentleman Teacher. The first graders, however, had not yet learned that song.

"How about 'Let's Study Hard' then? The first graders know it too." Gentleman Teacher wanted the pupils to sing what he had taught them. Masuno, however, shouted promptly "'A Mountain Crow'!"

It really seemed to be her favorite song. She started singing it right away.

"*A mountain crow brought me*
    A small, red envelope."

Although she was only in the first grade, she already seemed competent and experienced in leading the chorus. Maybe she was born that way. She was quite capable of making the others follow her in singing.

"*I opened it, and read*
    Of a great forest fire
    Under the shining moon."

In the meantime, a crowd of villagers had gathered and made their farewells. Miss Oishi got onto the boat, singing with the children.

"*I meant to answer it,*
    But from my dream awoke.
    And by my bed there lay
    A small, red maple leaf."

The song was repeated again and again, until it finally stopped without their realizing it. The children called to the boat which was moving farther and farther away. They went on calling while their voices gradually became inaudible.

" Teacher ! "

" Come again."

" Come back when your foot gets well."

" It's a promise."

" IT'S A PROMISE." The last was Nita's voice. They still kept on calling, but Miss Oishi could no longer make out the words.

" Aren't they cute ! " The ferryman spoke to her, waking her from her reverie. Still keeping her eyes on the people who seemed reluctant to leave the beach, she said, " Yes, they are all very nice."

" Yet we always hear the people there are hard to get along with."

" That's right. But that kind of people are the nicest after they get to know you very well."

Exposing her face to the bright sun and sea breeze, Miss Oishi still fixed her eyes on the people who looked as small as sesame seeds now. It was as though she wanted to print the whole village deeply on her mind. Far out at sea, where nothing was heard any more, except the sound of the scull, the singing of the children seemed to return to her ear. Their round, shining eyes, too, remained vivid in her memory.

5

The Picture of a Flower

Both the color of the sea and the shape of the hills were the same as before. The group of children walking along the long, narrow cape path to school was moving at the same place at the same time as before. A closer observation, however, would have revealed some new faces, and, perhaps because of them, the expressions of the children were as fresh as the buds on the trees around them. Among them were Takeichi, Isokichi, Kichiji, with Masuno and Sanae following along behind. But from these new faces, it must be realized that four years had passed since the beginning of our story. Was life for these children, under the slogan "A hundred million countrymen united," the same as four years before? Unchanged like the shape of the hills and the color of the sea around their village?

The children did not think about this kind of thing. They were just growing up with their own joys and sorrows. They grew naturally, without realizing that they had been placed in the midst of a great current of history. Significant events had taken place during the past four years, but the children were all too young to really understand their meanings. Yet history was being made outside the scope of these little children's minds. Four years before, on the fifteenth of March, 1928, a little before these children entered the branch school in the cape village, and again on the sixteenth of April of the next year, immediately after they were moved up to the second grade, many fellow Japanese who demanded freedom for the people and planned reforms had been put into jail by the government which suppressed progressive ideas. The cape children, however, knew nothing of this. All that was deeply impressed on their minds was the depression. Although they did not know it was a world-wide phenomenon, they understood one thing clearly : that the depression had come though through no fault of theirs and everyone had to be frugal. They had heard about the famine in Northern Honshu and in Hokkaido, and each had brought a donation of one sen to school. Then the Manchuria and Shanghai incidents had occurred one after the other and several men from the cape had been drafted.

While these events were happening in rapid succession, the little children ate rice mixed with barley and grew up bright and cheerful. They did not know what lay ahead. They were just happy to grow.

They were fifth graders now, but their parents could not afford to buy them sneakers, which were now the fashion. Yet they did not complain, blaming the depression over which they had no control. The children contented themselves with traditional straw sandals, and their spirits were light because they were wearing new ones today. Still, when they found that Tadashi alone had on sneakers, they stared at them and made a fuss about them.

"Wow, Tanko! Aren't your feet bright! They blind me."

Tadashi had been shy about his sneakers from the first. Now that his friends had mentioned them, he was so embarrassed that he regretted wearing them.

Among the girls, Kotsuru was the only one with sneakers. They were so big that they almost came off at each step. She finally picked them up in her hands and looked at them ruefully, standing barefoot. A sixth grade girl, offering to change them for her sandals, commented loudly: " My, they're size seven —too big even for me! "

Kotsuru's parents had probably bought them in hopes that she could use them for three years or so. Kotsuru did not want to have anything more to do with the new sneakers. Slipping into the sandals, it was much easier to walk. As she gave a sigh of relief, Matsue addressed her smiling, " Look, Kotsuru.

My lunch here is still very warm," and patted the box she carried at her side.

" One with a lily on it? " asked Kotsuru with a How-did-you-ever-get-one? look on her face.

Matsue answered, " No, Dad's going to buy it tomorrow."

She was startled at her own reply. What had happened three days before suddenly came back to her. She had heard that Misako and Masuno had gotten alumite lunch boxes with pictures of lilies on the lids, and she had asked her mother, " Mahchan and Miisan both got lunch boxes with lilies. Please buy me one like theirs soon."

" Okay."

" Will you really? "

" Sure I will."

" One with a lily, huh? "

" A lily, a chrysanthemum, or anything you like."

" Will you ask the bellman soon? "

" Okay, but don't be in such a rush."

" But all you say is ' Okay.' Shall I go tell the bellman now? "

That finally made her mother take her seriously. Without saying " Okay " this time, she said, talking a little quickly: " Wait a second now. Who's going to pay for it? You must wait until Dad makes enough money. We'd lose face otherwise. I'll find you a nice lunch box now—much nicer than an alumite one."

Thus Matsue was talked out of it. But when her mother showed her the old wicker lunch box she had found for her, she burst out crying in disappointment. She knew that wicker lunch boxes had long since become unpopular and that no one carried them any more. The depression had affected her father's business too, and whenever he had no carpentering to do, he took odd jobs, such as weeding. Matsue knew, therefore, that even a lunch box was not an easy thing for him to buy. Still she wanted one very badly. She had the feeling that if she accepted the wicker one now, she would never get one with a lily. So she remained adamant and finally began crying. However, her mother would not give in either.

"It's the depression, you see. Have a little patience. If Dad's business gets better next month, we'll really buy you one. You're the oldest child, Matsue, and you must be more understanding."

But the girl went on sobbing. Her disappointment was so great that she had kept on obstinately as though she would never stop. Then something intervened, something quite serious. "Matsu," her mother said firmly, "I promise to buy you a lunch box. I swear. But now I want you to run to the midwife's. Ask her to come right away. On your way there stop by at the general store and ask the old lady to come, too. Funny I should be feeling this way."

She muttered the last part of it to herself and started spreading her bed in the back room. Matsue, seeing her mother do this, stopped crying, stubborn as she was, and hurried out of the house. The small girl ran as fast as an arrow, a pleasant expectation swelling up in her chest. Her mother's promise had given her hope.

The midwife's house was located at the entrance to the principal village. The woman gave the girl a ride on her bicycle part of the way back. When they came to a slightly upward slope, the old midwife stopped her bicycle and said, " You get off here. I have to go as fast as I can."

Matsue nodded and started running after the bicycle, which was moving off swiftly and soon disappeared into the hills. Since Miss Oishi's bicycle, women riding bicycles had gradually increased in number, and they were no longer curiosities. Watching the midwife's bicycle speeding away, it flashed into Matsue's mind how much it would help her father to have one like that. He had to get up early every morning and trudge to town to go to work.

When she arrived home running, the baby had already been born. The general store proprietress, who was busy drawing water, her kimono sleeves

tucked up with a cord, said to Matsue as soon as she
saw her. " Matchan, sorry to put you to work, but
will you make a fire under the pot at once? "

After pouring water from a bucket into the pot, she
spoke in a low voice: " It's a very small girl—a
premature baby. But it doesn't matter, does it, Matchan? Your dad may be disappointed to see another
girl, but it's nice to have girls. Girls can't serve in
the military like boys, but who can tell if you won't
rise in the world in ten years or so? "

Matsue did not understand what the old woman
meant, and just kept on feeding the fire under the
pot. Whenever there was something wrong with
her mother, Matsue had to do the cooking, because
she did not have a grandmother to do the job. It
had been that way since she had been very little.

Today, three days later, was the first day Matsue
had ever been to the main school—and that with a
lunch. She had been filling lunch boxes with the
steaming rice from the pot, while her mother gave her
instructions from her bed in the back room.

" Put as much rice as you can into Daddy's box.
Don't fill yours, though. It's a big box, you know.
Push a pickled plum well into the rice so that it won't
show. Otherwise it would make a hole in the lid."

Matsue's mother, a hand towel wrapped around her
aching head, was close to delirium with the pain she

bore. She grimaced. The little girl, however, paid
no attention to her mother's discomfort.

" Mother, will you really buy me a lunch box with
a lily? When will you buy it?"

" As soon as I'm up."

" On the day you can get up?"

" Sure."

Matsue was so happy today that she did not mind
the size of her father's aluminum lunch box she had
borrowed to take to school. It was a large, deep
box that would contain enough food for three girls
of Matsue's age, but it did not occur to her how
funny it would look in a primary school classroom.
She preferred it to the wicker box. Besides, the lunch
box kept not only her body but her heart pleasantly
warm. To Kotsuru's question Matsue had answered
" Tomorrow," without thinking, but tomorrow was
too early. " I may get it day after tomorrow, though,"
she thought to herself, smiling. She walked on with
this feeling in her heart. All the other children, too,
were happy about things of their own. Masuno was
proud of the new sailor blouse she had on; Kotoe
liked the red bands on the sandals Grandma had made
for her; Sanae, who had on a lined kimono with small
white checks—quiet patterns that might better befit
a college age girl—, could not refrain from thinking

of the red lining and looking down occasionally at
the sleeve of her kimono. When she had first tried
it on, her mother had told her before anyone had had a
chance to criticize it for being too conservative: " I
was afraid it might look too old for you, but the red
lining improves it a lot. It's very becoming, Sanae.
You look smart in it. The way the lining shows a
little at the sleeve is just right. It's wonderful, and
I'm so glad."

Because her mother had admired the kimono so
much, Sanae readily believed her. Sanae and Kotoe
were the only two who had kimonos on. Kotoe's
kimono, like Sanae's, must have belonged to her
mother. It was dark cotton with white designs here
and there. It had not been recut, and the tucks at
the shoulders and hip were quite conspicuous. Her
sandals with red bands, however, gave her real pride.
When the children passed the bush by the bamboo
grove, Kotoe alone happened to think of Miss Oishi
and looked across to the Pine Tree village where she
lived.

" Miss Koishi ! " Kotoe said her teacher's nickname secretly to herself, but Kotsuru approached her
as if she had heard it.

" Do you know the news about Miss Koishi ? "

" What's that ? "

Seeing that Kotoe did not know, Kotsuru asked

Sanae next, " Do you know, Sanae? "

" What? "

Looking from one child to another, Kotsuru asked loudly, " Do you know the news about Miss Koishi? "

News always came from Kotsuru. Immediately the children surrounded her. Kotsuru stared proudly at each of them in turn with those narrow eyes of hers which never opened wide even when she stared.

" Miss Koishi . . . she . . . Something nice has happened to her." And she whispered something into Masuno's ear. She meant it to be a secret just between Masuno and herself, but Masuno exclaimed in an excited voice, " Boy, she got married ! "

" And then," Kotsuru made an intentional pause there, suggesting that she had something more to say. "For the hooneymon . . . er . . . honeyman . . . well anyway they went to . . . er . . . Don't you wanna know? "

" Sure I do ! "

" Me too ! "

" K-O-M-P-I-R-A."

" I get it. They went to Kompira Shrine."

" That's right."

They began shouting with excitement. The upperclass boys, who had gotten about a hundred yards ahead of them, looked back but kept on going. The fifth graders followed them, quickening their pace; yet they went on talking loudly about " Mrs. Oishi."* They found out that the wedding had taken place two days ago, and that Kotsuru's father had brought the news yesterday. It was Masuno's opinion that now that Mrs. Oishi had been married she might quit school. Kotsuru agreed and reminded the others that Miss Kobayashi, the former teacher, had resigned in order to get married. Masuno was also the first to say that she would like Mrs. Oishi to stay. For once, Sanae and Kotoe agreed.

" We'd like to see Miss Koishi again, wouldn't we? " Sanae spoke to Kotsuru.

" Sure. Didn't those noodles, that time, taste good? " Kotoe said. The others began to remember clearly what had happened four years before, and, all of a sudden, it was a serious question for them whether Mrs. Oishi would be at school today. Unconsciously they quickened their steps. Half running, Masuno suggested, " Shall we bet? Will Miss Koishi be at school or not? "

" Okay. What do you want to bet? " responded Kotsuru without a moment's hesitation.

" If you lose, you'll . . . er . . . er . . . get five slaps

---

* Since Miss Oishi was an only child and had no brother to carry on her family name, her husband had been adopted into her family. Thus by the process of marriage, she had become merely *Mrs*. Oishi.

on your hand," said Tadashi.

"I don't mind losing then. I bet she's there," said Masuno, raising her right hand up high.

"Me too."

"Me too."

In the end, they all thought Mrs. Oishi would be there, and the bet was canceled. In the meantime, they were getting near the school. Being newcomers, the fifth graders looked serious as they went through the gate. Then, glancing up, they noticed Mrs. Oishi looking their way out of the window of the faculty room. She waved at them to come nearer, and they ran toward her.

"I've been anxiously waiting for you. Just a minute," she said and came out of the room. She led them to the river bank, walking in front of them. Looking at them one after another, she said, "You've all grown very tall. You'll catch up with me pretty soon. My, Kotsuru, you're almost taller than I."

She stood by Kotsuru's side. "You win. But I can't do anything about it. I'm Koishi after all."

They all laughed.

"Because you nicknamed me Miss Koishi, I can never be Oishi."

They laughed again but still did not say anything.

"Aren't you quiet! Are you so quiet because you're fifth graders now?"

Still they just smiled, because Mrs. Oishi somehow looked a little different from before. Her skin had become fairer, and there was a fragrant smell about her like a violet's. They knew it was the way a bride would smell.

"Teacher," said Masuno at last. "Are you going to teach us music?"

"Yes. Not only music, though. I'll be your homeroom teacher this year."

The children gave a shout of joy and began talking all at once, vying for her attention, calling, "Teacher! Teacher!" They filled her with their talk of happenings in the cape village and she saw again in her mind's eye the houses, the color of the sea, and heard the sound of the wind and the surf. Kotoe's grandfather had died of apoplexy recently; Isokichi's mother was laid up with rheumatism; Sanae had gotten scratched on her forehead the other day when she and Misako had been skipping with their arms around each other's shoulders and fallen off the road onto the beach; at Kitchin's, three pigs had died of pigs' cholera and now his mother was sick in bed. . . . The children's stories never seemed to end.

Kotsuru clung to the teacher and shook her. "Teacher, do you know why Nita didn't come?"

"Oh, I meant to ask you. What's the matter with him? Is he sick?"

The children did not answer right away but looked at each other, smiling. Mrs. Oishi was tempted to smile too. It suddenly occurred to her that Nita must have done something extraordinary.

"What's wrong with him? Is he sick?" Mrs. Oishi asked Sanae, but the girl shook her head without a word and looked down.

"He flunked," replied Misako.

"Oh, really?" The teacher was taken aback. As if to make her laugh, Kotsuru said, "Because he always has a runny nose."

The children laughed, but Mrs. Oishi did not.

"That's not true. If a runny nose made you flunk, you'd all have flunked at the end of the first year. Maybe Nita cut too many classes because of illness or something."

"But that's what Gentleman Teacher said," explained Kotsuru. " ' Runny noses are usually excused, but Nita's nose has been running for four years and never seems to stop. That's why he has to stay in the fourth grade,' Gentleman Teacher said."

At this, the children all snuffled. That made the teacher smile for a second, but she immediately looked anxious again. The bell announced the beginning of school, and she said good-by to the pupils. Going back to the faculty room, she thought about nothing but Nita. "Poor child," she muttered. The thought

that Nita had flunked and would have to go over the
same course again with his brother Sankichi, depressed
her. She wondered if Gentleman Teacher had really
made that comment about runny noses. She was
afraid that keeping Nita back a class would only make
his nose keep on running. If the naiveté of that big
boy, Nita, were lost as a result of this, it would be a
life-long misfortune for him, Mrs. Oishi thought.
She could feel Nita's loneliness for being left behind
all alone today. She kept repeating to herself, "Runny
noses are usually excused," and still she could not figure
out why Nita had flunked.

After lunch, Mrs. Oishi went outdoors to ask
Takeichi about the matter. She stood under the
willow tree on the river bank overlooking the playground. Takeichi was not to be seen. Instead she
caught sight of Matsue, who, for some reason, was
standing forlornly by herself against the wall of the
schoolhouse. When Mrs. Oishi beckoned her, she
came running to the bottom of the bank. Smiling,
Matsue's eyes looked exactly like her mother's. The
teacher gave her a hand, and the girl let herself be pulled
up; her bashful expression reminded Mrs. Oishi of
her mother even more. Not realizing that Mrs.
Oishi wanted to ask her about Nita, Matsue addressed
her seriously as if she could no longer bear her loneliness.

" Teacher."

" Yes ? "

" Er-r-r. . . . My mother had a baby girl."

" Oh, did she? Congratulations! What's her name? "

" Well, she hasn't got a name yet. She was born only day before yesterday. Tomorrow, day after to-morrow, two days after tomorrow. . . ." She slowly counted on her fingers. " She'll be named two days from tomorrow. This time I'm supposed to think up a nice name."

" Are you? Have you already thought up one? "

" Not yet. I was thinking just now." Matsue chuckled happily.

" Teacher," she addressed Mrs. Oishi again as if she wanted to talk about something else this time.

" Yes? You sound happy, don't you? What is it? "

" Er. . . . Mummy says she'll buy me an alumite lunch box when she gets up—the kind of box that has a picture of a lily on the lid." Matsue breathed in with a little sound, a smile spreading all over her face.

"A lunch box with a picture of a lily? Isn't that wonderful! Oh, are you going to name the baby after lilies, too? "

" I don't know yet."

" You don't? Make up your mind now. Name her

after lilies. Yuriko? Yurie?* I like Yurie better. There are too many Yurikos these days."

Matsue nodded and looked up at the teacher happily. It seemed to Mrs. Oishi as though she had noticed the tenderness of her eyes for the first time, and she fondly looked at her black eyes shaded with long eye-lashes. Despite her worries about Nita, Mrs. Oishi, before she knew it, began to feel happy. Matsue, on her part, was several times happier than the teacher. Although she did not tell Mrs. Oishi, she had been ridiculed at lunch time by Kotsuru and Misako because of her father's big lunch box. That was why she had been standing apart from her friends. But now she had recovered her spirits just as wilted grass revives with the dew on a summer morning. She was happy with the thought that Mrs. Oishi had been particularly nice to her, and decided not to mention this to anyone.

On her way home that day, however, she carelessly referred to it.

" We're going to name the baby Yurie."

" Yurie? Hmm, Yuriko sounds better," retorted Kotsuru.

Matsue expanded her chest. " But Miss Koishi said Yurie was better because it was less common."

Kotsuru pretended to be surprised. " What ! Why

---

* *Yuri* means *lily ;* *ko* and *e* are suffixes for female names.

Miss Koishi? I wonder." She peered at Matsue's face with scrutinizing eyes. " Oh, I see," she said. She then pulled back Misako, who had been walking by her side, and whispered to her. She whispered something to Fujiko, Sanae and Kotoe in turn and asked, " Don't you think so? "

The three quiet girls, however, expressed their disagreement by timid silence, so that Kotsuru failed in her plot to isolate Matsue. It was disadvantageous for Kotsuru that Masuno, who always agreed with her, was stopping by at her mother's restaurant today and was not there. Kotsuru had told the girls that Masuno must have flattered Mrs. Oishi in order to be specially favored. As a result, Kotsuru, having been ignored, walked ahead of the others in bad-tempered silence. They followed her quietly.

As they came around a bend, Kotsuru suddenly stood still in front of them and looked toward the sea. Like wild geese following their leader, the others looked in the same direction. When Kotsuru started to walk again, the others followed. But after a while, with their eyes fixed on the sea, they forgot to go on.

Had Kotsuru known it from the beginning? Or had she noticed it just now like her friends? Over the calm spring sea went a fishing boat at a high speed. Two half-naked men with hand towels around their heads were sculling the boat with all their might. The boat was hurrying toward the town across the bay, the sculls leaving a broad belt of white foam behind. The girls left out their quarreling.

" What could that be ? "

" Is there anything wrong with someone's family ? "

They looked at one another. From the white belt of foam continuously trailing behind the boat, they judged that an accident had occurred in the cape village. Someone must have been taken suddenly ill. They saw a bed spread on the boat and guessed that someone must be lying on it. The boat, however, went away so fast that it was impossible to make out who was on board. It went by like a momentary dream, but they all knew that it was not a dream. They looked back to the emergencies in the past. Once every one or two years there had been urgent cases to be carried to the hospital in town. Once Mrs. Oishi, too, had been sent that way. Would today's case be an injury or acute appendicitis?

" What could that be ? "

" I wonder if someone had appendicitis."

The boys had caught up with the girls and discussed various possibilities, standing in a group. The girls remained quiet and looked at whichever boy said something. Matsue, in the meantime, remembered how her mother had looked when she had left home that morning. For an instant, she was seized with

anxiety, as though a black shadow had overcast her
mind, but she strongly rejected it, telling herself that
it could not be. Yet she could not help feeling
anxious when she recalled her mother's grimace of
that morning. She had tied her hand towel so tightly
around her head in order to fight off the headache
that the knot had formed deep wrinkles on her forehead. At first, she had asked her husband not to go
to work, but he could not possibly afford to miss a
day.

"Let Matsue stay home," he said.

"Never mind then," replied Matsue's mother and
then spoke to her. "This is the first day of school,
isn't it? You may go, but come directly home, will
you?"

Now that Matsue had been reminded of this, her
heart began beating fast. Before she knew it, she was
running ahead of the others. They ran after her.
Matsue ran and ran until she almost tumbled from
fatigue. By the time she reached the place from
where the rows of village houses could be seen, her
knees were shaking under her, and she was gasping for
breath. The general store was the nearest house, and
beyond it was her house. She was relieved to see the
baby's diapers fluttering in the air. The sense of
relief made her almost cry, but at the next moment
her heart nearly stopped beating; for she found that

it was not her mother but the general store proprietress who was by the well. She ran down the hill like a bounding stone, dashed into her house, and rushed into the backroom at the same speed. Her mother was supposed to be there, but she was not.

" Mother ! "

No one answered.

" Mother ! " she cried tearfully. In the direction of the general store a baby was heard crying.

" Oh, oh ! Mother ! " She screamed with all her might, her voice reaching up to the sky and out to the sea.

6

Crabs and the Moon

The fifth grade classroom was next to the entrance of the newly built schoolhouse, looking out on the river. Outside the windows was a narrow, triangular vacant lot, and beyond it was a high stone embankment built perpendicular to the river bed. A bank, three feet from the ground, had been built to prevent accidents, but it did not serve the purpose, for the children felt free to climb down the stone embankment to the river even during the short recesses. They were mostly boys. The trickling water was clean, because there were no houses upstream. It originated in the mountains and remained surprisingly cold and pure until it got to the school, where it was touched by human beings for the first time. The children were completely satisfied and pleased just to touch the water with their hands and feet. It was here that the stream was touched, interrupted, and made impure. Ever since someone had spread the rumor that there were eels around, the children's enthusiasm had been concentrated on the river bed, and there had been constant argument between the

spectators on the banks and the fishermen in the river
every day. The children turned over the stones in
the river bed, hunting for eels that had never been
caught. All they could find were crabs. Still it
seemed to be lots of fun; consequently, the number
of fishermen and spectators increased day by day.
The water was only about ankle-deep and was not
dangerous to play in. So Mrs. Oishi looked on
tolerantly.

"Mrs. Oishi, shall I give you a crab?" Tadashi
stretched his arm toward her, holding a crab with
coarse hair on its legs, protectively colored a muddy-
brown.

"I don't want that thing."

"But you can eat it."

"I don't want to. If I ate it, hair would grow on
my legs and arms."

There was a burst of laughter both from the river
bed and the bank. Needless to say, Mrs. Oishi,
standing by the window, laughed a great deal too.
Until just a while ago, however, she had been looking
at what was happening outdoors, feeling far from
gay. Unconsciously the children from the cape had
grouped together in the river as well as on the bank.
Among them, the teacher was unable to find Matsue,
and the image of the absent girl occupied her mind
from time to time.

Since her mother's death, Matsue had never shown up in the classroom. Her seat by the window, the third from the front, had been vacant for two months. It was about a month after her mother's death that Mrs. Oishi had visited Matsue's home. She had remembered what the girl had told her on the first day of school, and had taken as a gift a lunch box with a picture of a lily on it. Her father, Carpenter Kawa-moto, had happened to be at home that day. Man that he was, he had wept, telling the teacher that he could not send his daughter to school and keep the baby, too. His reasoning was so irrefutable that Mrs. Oishi was unable to press him any more and looked at Matsue without a word. The girl, with the little baby strapped to her back, sat shyly by her father's side and remained quiet. Her eyelids seemed swollen, and she had a vacant look as if her mind had stopped working. The teacher put the lunch box on her lap, saying, " Matchan, this is the lunch box you wanted. Use it when you can come to school again."

Matsue nodded expressionlessly.

" I hope you can come to school soon," Mrs. Oishi was startled at her own words, for what she had said could have meant that she hoped the baby would die soon. She blushed in spite of herself, but Matsue and her father did not seem hurt; they merely listened to her with grateful looks in their eyes.

A little later, Mrs. Oishi learned that the baby had died, and felt relieved for Matsue. But the girl still did not come to school. The teacher asked Masuno and Kotoe about her, but was unable to get any satisfactory information. Finally she wrote her a letter. That had been about ten days ago.

" Dear Matsue,

I was terribly sorry to hear about your baby sister, Yurie. But we cannot do anything for her any more. All we can do now is to cherish her memory in our hearts. Please cheer up. When are you coming back to school? I think of you every day, looking at your vacant seat.

Please come back to us soon, Matchan. Come and study with us."

Mrs. Oishi sent the letter by Kotoe, who lived nearest to Matsue. She knew, however, that in it she was asking Matsue to do the impossible. Even after the baby's death, the girl still had a brother and a sister, both younger than she. Although Matsue had just been moved up to the fifth grade and was still a little child mentally and physically, she was compelled to do the house-keeping. Much as she might dislike the job, there was no way out. In order to enable her father to go to work, little Matsue had to cook and wash. Mrs. Oishi pictured the three poor little children flocking together like chickens, waiting for their

father to come home from work. The law prescribed
that these children should be sent to school, but there
was no practical way of enforcing it.

The day after Mrs. Oishi had sent the letter, Kotoe
reported to her as soon as she saw her: " Teacher,
when I took your letter to Matchan's yesterday, there
was a woman I had never seen before. I asked her,
' Is Matchan home?' and she said, 'No, she isn't.'
So I had to give her the letter and asked her to give it
to Matchan."

"I see. Thank you very much. Was Matchan's
father home?"

"I don't know. I didn't see him. That woman
had her face powdered, and she was wearing a beautiful
kimono. Kotsuru says she may be Matchan's new
mother." Kotoe smiled bashfully.

"If it's true, Matchan will be able to come to school,"
the teacher said.

More than ten days had passed since then; still there
was no sign of Matsue. Looking down from the
window now, watching the children at crabbing, Mrs.
Oishi wondered anxiously if the girl had read her
letter.

Tadashi came up the embankment proudly, carrying
three crabs he had caught in an empty can. With
summer approaching, the apricot tree in the triangular
vacant lot, thick with green leaves, cast its dark shadow

on the bank. The girls from the cape, gathering under the tree, welcomed the crab hunter, each of them striving to be the first to speak to him.

"Tanko, give me one, will you?"

"Give me one, too."

"Me too, huh?"

"Promise?"

There were only three crabs to four girls. Tadashi climbed to the top of the embankment, still thinking.

"Are you going to eat them or not?" He looked around at each of the girls. He thought he would give the crabs to those who would eat them. Kotsuru answered before anyone else: "I sure am. Crabs taste good after moonlit nights, you know."

Tadashi grinned at this. "You liar! It's after moonless nights that they taste good."

"You liar! It's after moonlit nights."

"I've never heard that. Don't you know crabs get thin and don't taste good after moonlit nights?" said Tadashi, convinced.

But Kotsuru would not give in and mimicked him. "I've never heard that. Don't you know crabs taste good after moonlit nights? I'll eat them to make sure. Give them all to me."

"No, you can't tell from these river crabs. You must have sea crabs."

This argument put the girls into an uproar.

" Teacher, which is right, ' moonlit ' or ' moonless ' ?
' Moonlit ' is right, isn't it ? " Masuno, Kotsuru, and
Misako all together asked the teacher by the window.

" Well. . . . I guess ' moonless ' is right."

The boys shouted for joy. " You see ! We told
you ! "

" But I'm not sure. Maybe ' moonlit ' is right,"
said the teacher, smiling this time.

The girls jumped happily with their hands up. No
one was serious, of course. They just enjoyed raising
a clamor that way. However, only Tadashi looked
up at the teacher in earnest. " Are you nuts ? "

The girls set up a great clamor again.

" You call your teacher nuts ? "

" My, he calls his teacher nuts ! "

Tadashi scratched his head. But when the others
had quieted down, he spoke to Mrs. Oishi just as
seriously as before. " But there's a reason for it.
Crabs are stupid, so on moonlit nights they mistake
their own shadows for ghosts. They're scared and
get thin. But on moonless nights, there aren't any
shadows, so they aren't afraid and get fat. That's
why we let them go if they get caught in a net on a
moonlit night. They're thin and don't taste good,
you see. If you wait until a moonless night, they get
so fat and tasty. I mean it, Teacher. If you don't
believe me, you'd better try them."

"All right, let's all try them then," answered Mrs. Oishi jokingly, thereby putting an end to the matter.

Two days later, however, Tadashi really brought sea crabs caught after a moonlit night. He held out his gourd-shaped basket when the first period of arithmetic began.

"Crabs, Teacher. Moonlit night crabs, thin and tasteless."

They had been caught only that morning and were still alive. They were rustling in the basket. The pupils laughed.

"Did you really bring them, Tanko?" smiled the teacher and received the basket reluctantly. The crabs were creeping around inside the basket with a rustling noise, as though they were striving desperately against their fate. They both had one of their big claws ripped off somehow and looked miserable. Lifting up the other claw, as though to nip anyone that might come within their reach, they were foaming at the mouth.

"Poor things! Am I supposed to eat them?"

"Sure, that's what you promised."

"Let's let them go."

"No, you've got to keep your promise."

Tadashi turned around and asked the others to

agree, saying "Right?" The boys clapped their hands in excitement.

"Let's do it this way then. How about asking the janitor to boil them later so that we can study them during the science class today? And for homework you write themes on crabs. How'll that be?"

"Okay!"

"Okay!"

The pupils all agreed whole-heartedly. The basket was hung on the nail by the window. The crabs kept rustling during the class, making the children laugh.

After the class, Mrs. Oishi took the basket off the nail and started for the janitor's room. Kotsuru and Kotoe followed her as if they had something to say.

"Teacher," they spoke to her. When the teacher turned around, they said, "Matchan . . ."

"Matchan?"

"Yes, she went to Osaka by boat last night."

"Oh, no!" The teacher stood still despite herself. Looking up at her, Kotoe said earnestly, "She was adopted by her relatives."

"Was she really?"

"And her daddy and brother stayed behind."

"I see. Was Matchan happy?"

Kotoe shook her head silently. Kotsuru spoke this time. "Matchan said she wouldn't go and clung to the gate post at first, crying. Her father didn't know what to do. First he tried to talk her into going, but she still held on to the post. So he finally hit her on the head and back with his fist. Matchan howled, and nobody knew what to do. The old lady of the general store finally talked her into going, and Matchan gave in. They all felt sorry for her and cried with her. So did I. I followed her part of the way with the others. Matchan didn't say a word to anybody. Isn't that right, Kotoe? And . . . ," she stopped there, surprised; for Mrs. Oishi had suddenly started to sob, putting her handkerchief on her face. Sanae and Masuno had joined the group in the meantime, and the girls all looked at their teacher sadly, who, her head drooping, held her handkerchief to her eyes, with the basket in her hand. Their eyes, too, filled with tears of sympathy.

For some time after this, Matsue's seat, the third from the front by the window, was kept vacant. One day, Mrs. Oishi was seen occupying that seat quietly, where the girl had sat just for one day. Soon after that, the seats were rearranged, and Matsue's seat was taken by a boy. No one talked about her any more. Mrs. Oishi did not ask about her; the pupils did not speak of her; and the girl did not write. It appeared that everyone had forgotten Matsue—that fifth grade girl who had gone away without even saying good-by.

It was early in March, a little before the children were moved up to the sixth grade. Spring was just around the corner; yet strangely it was snowing that day. Mrs. Oishi missed the usual bus and had to take a later one. She ran from the bus stop to the school without even putting up her umbrella and entered the faculty room hurriedly. Then something in the atmosphere of the room made her stop short. She looked around at the fifteen teachers, wondering whom she should speak to. They all looked anxious and stiff.

"What's up?" she asked her colleague, Miss Tamura. As if to tell her to hush, Miss Tamura pointed with her chin to the principal's room in the back and whispered, "Mr. Kataoka was taken to the police."

"Oh, no!"

Again, Miss Tamura shook her head quickly, cautioning Mrs. Oishi to be quiet. "They're there now." Miss Tamura winked at the principal's room and whispered that they had been searching Mr. Kotaoka's desk until just a minute ago. None of the teachers seemed to know what it was all about. They just sat around the brazier silently. When the school bell rang, they went out into the hall, breathing freely again. Mrs. Oishi went into the hall with Miss Tamura and asked her impatiently, "What was the matter?"

" They say he's a ' Red.' "

" ' Red '? Why? "

" I don't know why."

" Is he a Red? Why? "

" I don't know. Don't ask me."

They had reached Mrs. Oishi's classroom and parted smiling, although it still seemed to them that there was something left to be discussed. The pupils, who apparently did not yet know anything about what had happened, looked more lively than usual, probably because of the snow. Mrs. Oishi tried to concentrate on her class, but the class hour had never seemed so long since she had started teaching five years ago. When she returned to the faculty room after the class, she found the teachers looking relieved.

" The police are gone," said a young bachelor, a graduate of a teachers' college, smiling. He went on to say, " This proves that sincerity never pays."

" What do you mean by that? " asked Mrs. Oishi. " Talk like a teacher." Someone poked her, making her stop talking. It was Miss Tamura.

The vice-principal came in and explained the situation. He said that Mr. Kataoka was only being questioned and would soon be back now that the principal had gone for him. According to him, the key man was not Mr. Kataoka but one Inagawa, a teacher of a primary school in a nearby town, who was said to have inspired his homeroom pupils with pacifism. Mr. Kataoka had been investigated because he had been a classmate of Mr. Inagawa's at teachers' college, but he had been exonerated; that is, the authorities had been unable to find evidence. By "evidence," they meant incriminating literature in the form of a collection of compositions entitled *The Seeds of Grass* written by Mr. Inagawa's sixth grade class. The police had failed to find a copy of it either in Mr. Kataoka's house or in his desk at school.

"Why, I've seen *The Seeds of Grass* myself, but how could that be 'red'?" asked Mrs. Oishi, puzzled.

The vice-principal smiled. "That only shows sincerity doesn't pay, you see. If the police heard you talk that way, they'd label you 'Red,' too."

"I don't understand that. You know, I liked some compositions in that pamphlet so much I once read them to my class. 'Wheat Harvest' and 'The Chimney of a Soy-sauce Factory' were good ones."

"Watch out, watch out! Did you get the pamphlet from Mr. Inagawa?"

"No, I just read the one that was sent to school."

The vice-principal asked hurriedly, "Where is it now?"

"In my homeroom."

"Get it right away, will you?"

The mimeographed pamphlet was immediately put

on the brazier and burned in haste, as though it had been contaminated by plague germs or something. Brownish smoke rose to the ceiling and escaped out of the slightly opened window.

"Oh, maybe I should have handed this to the police instead of burning it. But they might have taken Mrs. Oishi then. Well, anyway we'd better remain loyal and patriotic subjects," said the vice-principal. Mrs. Oishi followed the smoke with her eyes without a word, as though she had not heard him.

The next day, the newspapers reported on Mr. Inagawa's case with eye-catching headlines which read: Red Teacher Spoils Innocent Minds. The local people were taken aback, as if they had been hit on their heads with a hammer. Mr. Inagawa, who was said to have been popular with his pupils, was suddenly degraded to a traitor's position.

"How horrible! We'd better be very conventional now," muttered the second head teacher, an old man. The other teachers did not say what they thought or how they felt. Mrs. Oishi read certain lines in the exaggerated newspaper article over and over again. The lines related how Mr. Inagawa's pupils had each brought an egg from home and had marched in a group to the police station where they insisted that the eggs be given to their teacher in the cold detention room.

Mr. Kataoka, who was back at school today, was deluged with questions, as if he had suddenly become a hero. "How was it?" asked someone. Mr. Kataoka answered, rubbing his cheeks which had become hollow in a day and were blue-black with the traces of his beard: "Awful! It was pure nonsense when I think of it now, but they almost labeled me 'Red.' They said, 'Inagawa says you attended their meetings four or five times.' They also said, 'You must have read Takiji Kobayashi's works.' So I said, 'I don't even know the name.' Then they said, 'Bastard, you must have read about him in the papers just recently.' That reminded me. Do you remember a novelist who died in prison just recently?" (Although actually he was tortured to death, it was reported in the newspaper that he had died of a heart attack.)

"Oh, yes, I remember that. He was a red novelist," answered the young bachelor teacher.

"The police confiscated lots of his books on the proletariat or something or other from Inagawa. He's been fond of reading since his college days," said Mr. Kataoka.

During Japanese class that day, Mrs. Oishi ventured something, because she was certain that her pupils already knew the news about Mr. Inagawa, the editor of *The Seeds of Grass.*

"How many of you take newspapers at home?"
she asked.

About one third of the forty-two pupils raised their
hands.

"How many of you read them?"

Only two or three hands were raised.

"Does anybody know what 'Red' means?"

No one raised his hand. They looked at one another with expressions of a vague knowledge which
they could not explain clearly.

"Does anybody know what 'proletariat' means?"

No one did.

"How about 'capitalists'?"

"I know." One hand was raised. When called
upon, the pupil answered, "They are rich people."

"Hmm. . . . Okay. What are workers then?"

"I know."

"I know."

Most of the pupils raised their hands. It was about
the only question that from their own experience they
could answer confidently. Mrs. Oishi was no different in that respect. If some pupil had asked her
answers to the other questions, she would have said,
"I don't know very well either." Anyway, the fifth
graders were still too young to really understand these
things.

Immediately afterwards, Mrs Oishi was told not to

talk about this sort of thing. Someone must have informed the principal of that innocent discussion, for she was called and warned by him. "Please be careful," he said. "We must watch our tongues nowadays, you know."

He did not take any further measures, probably because he favored the daughter of his old friend. But this incident, together with the case of *The Seeds of Grass*, which she had thought harmless, gave the otherwise gay Mrs. Oishi a depressed look, which not only stayed with her but grew even more conspicuous with time.

In the meantime, Mrs. Oishi's pupils progressed to the sixth grade. In the fall of that year, it was decided, in view of the times, that they should take a trip to Kompira, which was nearer than Ise, the usual destination of the annual sixth grade excursion. Even then there were quite a few who found it difficult to participate. In the country, people were as thrifty as they were hard-working. Some of the parents consented later on the condition that the children would not stay overnight at an inn and would take three lunches along. Still it was only about 60 per cent of the eighty pupils, two sections put together, who could go. The children from the cape village especially did not commit themselves until very late. They found out how things stood with one another, and then told Mrs. Oishi.

"Teacher, Sonki can't go because he wets his bed at night," said Masuno.

"But, you see, we won't stay overnight at an inn. We'll take a morning boat over and come back on an evening boat."

"But the boat will leave at 4 a.m. Won't we sleep in the boat?"

"I wonder. It's only a two-hour trip, and you'll all be too excited to sleep, I guess. By the way, why aren't *you* going, Masuno?"

"Because I might catch cold."

"What a coddled child!"

"My parents will save twice as much money for me as the cost of the trip, though."

"They will? But they can save money for you some other time, can't they? You'd better ask them to send you on the trip."

"But I'm afraid of an accident."

"Why? If we're afraid of colds or accidents, none of us can go on a trip."

"You'd better quit—all of you."

"Oh, you're just impossible." Mrs. Oishi forced a smile.

"Mrs. Oishi, I've already been to Kompira three

times by my father's boat. So I'm not going this time," said Tadashi.

"Aren't you? But you've never been there with your friends, have you? Your father's a head fisherman, so you'll have a chance to go there every year. But this time's special, so do come with us, Tadashi. I'm sure you'll remember this excursion as the best trip you ever took to Kompira."

Kotsuru was not going either, nor was Fujiko. Kotsuru explained, " Teacher, Fujiko's family is very much in debt, so she can't possibly go on the excursion. Her house is big, but it's mortgaged, so it'll soon be taken over. They have nothing left to sell in the whole house."

"Don't say things like that." Mrs. Oishi tapped Kotsuru on the back. Kotsuru put out her tongue.

"You bad girl!" As she was saying this, Mrs. Oishi remembered Fujiko's house. As early as the time of her first assignment to the cape, she had heard that the house might be handed over to someone else any day. She recalled the storehouse the plaster of which had completely come off on the north side. Fujiko, the child of an old family, was calm and serene—an attitude befitting her good lineage. She seldom either cried or smiled. Whenever Kotsuru, for instance, talked ill of her openly, she would stare

back at her coldly, which no one else had the courage
to do. She had a nickname " Rotten Bream," which
originated from her father's favorite proverb, " A
bream is the king of fish even when it's rotten," but
she did not seem to mind very much.

Kotsuru, on the other hand, was frank and open-
minded; she did not hesitate to speak ill of others,
nor did she mind particularly when others criticized
her. Her whole family worked hard, taking their sole
pride in it, and remained honest and frank.

Kotsuru had a nickname " Scarred Eyelid," because
she had had a boil on her eyelid once, which had left
a little mark there. Ordinary children, especially
girls, would have felt like crying if called " Scarred
Eyelid " teasingly. But Kotsuru was different. She
would reply without any shyness, as if it concerned
someone else: " Don't abuse that name. This is a
very special eye, and you can't have one like this so
easily." Probably she had learned that argument from
her parents.

This time, too, she told the teacher frankly why she
could not participate in the excursion. " My father
borrowed money from the mutual financing association
recently and bought a big boat. So we must econo-
mize. I've decided to visit Kompira when I get old
enough to earn my own money."

Being the kind of girl she was, Kotsuru poked her

nose into other people's purses and talked about them even if she was told not to. She would say, for instance, that Misako was not going because her family was stingy, and that Kotoe and Sanae could not possibly go because they had too many brothers and sisters.

Two days before the trip, however, the number of participants suddenly increased, and all the children from the cape, except Masuno, were now going.

This turn of events was brought about when the quiet Kichiji withdrew his savings earned by working in the woods, and used them to pay his fare. Isokichi immediately followed suit. He also had saved the commission he had earned by peddling bean curds, raw and fried. Now that Isokichi too was going, how could Tadashi and Takeichi stay at home? Tadashi thought of his savings earned by helping to draw in the nets; Takeichi said he would use the money he had earned by selling eggs. They lived in such a frugal village that they had not even thought of drawing out their savings for such a purpose. Tadashi's parents told him he did not need to do this, but he insisted and went to the post office himself with Takeichi.

The boys having come to this decision, the girls too had to do something about it. Misako, whose family was least hard up, invited Fujiko, because their mothers were good friends. A mother-of-pearl ink-stone case was transferred to Misako's house without Fujiko's knowledge. That made it possible for Fujiko to go on the trip. When Kotsuru heard about these two girls, she became impatient and started fussing at once.

"Miisan and Fujiko are going on the excursion. You've got to let me go too." Kotsuru really meant it, stamping her feet and crying until her narrow eyes were even narrower and swollen. Her mother laughed, narrowing her eyes that resembled Kotsuru's. The proposal she now made her daughter was a difficult one. "Miisan's family is rich, and Fujiko's father, after all, is a squire. We can't do everything they do. But if Kotoe's going, we'll let you go too. Go and see her about it." She said this, assuming that Kotoe could not possibly go. But Kotsuru promptly ran off and came back, smiling.

"Kotoe's going," she said, panting.

"Are you sure?"

"Yup, her mother was there and she told me."

It sounded so simple that Kotsuru's mother had doubts and went over to make sure. She suspected that Kotsuru, being so forward, might have talked her friend's family into it.

"Kotsuru didn't push you into it, did she?" she asked searchingly.

Kotoe's mother, as sunburnt as any fisherman,

grinned, showing her white teeth. " This kind of chance comes just once in a lifetime. Let's let them go. Kotoe usually works so hard, taking care of the younger children, you know."

" Kotsuru is no different. But what are you going to give Kotoe to put on? "

" I've decided to buy her a sailor blouse."

" They're pretty expensive, though, aren't they? "

" Don't hesitate this time. Buy one for Kotsuru too. Her kid sisters can wear it later, you know."

" Hmm."

" Sanae's going to have a sailor blouse too. So you'd better make up you mind to buy one for your daughter."

" I see. Sanae too, huh? Now I see why Kotsuru is so impatient. Oh dear! We'll have to do our best to send her."

That was how things went. At the last minute, however, Sanae withdrew her application because of " a touch of cold." But actually she had neither a sore throat nor a stuffed-up nose. It was her mother's purse that had gone wrong. She had gone to sell her ornamental hairpin with a coral head for her daughter, but had failed to sell it at the price she had in mind. Consequently she was unable to buy her daughter a blouse. She cursed the second-hand dealer, saying

that he had taken advantage of her circumstances.
To Sanae, however, she spoke tenderly. " Will you
go in a kimono? "

Sanae was on the verge of crying.

" Shall I tuck up your big sister's pretty kimono for
you? " her mother asked again. Sanae said nothing.

" If you don't want to be the only one going in a
kimono, don't go. It's either the trip or the blouse.
What do you say? "

Sanae shed tears, and her tightly closed lips
quivered. She could not decide which to choose.
But, as soon as she saw that her mother was moved
almost to tears herself, she made up her mind. " I'm
not going," she said.

The group of sixty-three went on the trip, none of
them knowing about these circumstances. Two men
and two women teachers, including Mrs. Oishi of
course, went along. After getting on the boat at
4 a.m., no one tried to go to sleep. Amid all the clamor,
some sang " A Boatride to Kompira."

In the meantime, Mrs. Oishi sat alone, brooding.
The thought of Sanae would not leave her mind.

Did she really have a cold? she wondered.

Besides Sanae, there were more than ten children
who did not go on the trip for various reasons.   Sanae
worried Mrs. Oishi particularly probably because she

was the only one from the cape who had not come. (Masuno no longer belonged to the cape village since she had moved to her parents' house in town.) When Mrs. Oishi thought of Sanae going along that cape path to school all by herself today, she felt sorry not to have called off the classes for the day. She pitied the other pupils, too, studying all alone in the teacher-less classroom.

They took the first train from Tadotsu and paid a morning visit to Kompira Shrine. Some sang " A Boatride to Kompira " again as they climbed the long flight of stone steps, sweating. Mrs. Oishi, on the other hand, shivered. The same kind of shiver attacked her again and again—on the train to Yashima and on the cable car there. She felt sick as though she had had cold water poured on her knees, and lost the serenity of mind necessary to enjoy the autumn scenery around her. All she did was to walk slowly into the souvenir shop and buy several sets of the same picture post cards because she wanted to bring something to the pupils who had been left behind.

They left Yashima and arrived in Takamatsu, their last stop. When they had their third lunch at the Chestnut Wood Park, Mrs. Oishi left most of hers untouched and asked the others to divide and finish it. She realized that until then even her lunch had weighed on her mind, and was relieved to have gotten rid of it. She walked with the others toward the port through the streets of Takamatsu, in the gathering dusk, longing desperately to go home and lie down and stretch her legs out. Miss Tamura spoke to her, " You look pale, Mrs. Oishi." This warning chilled her even more.

" I feel tired somehow. I feel awfully chilly."

" Isn't that a shame! Have you had any medicine? "

" I've been taking sedative pills called ' Cooling Pills,' " answered Mrs. Oishi, chuckling at their name. " But maybe I'd better not *cool* myself any more but eat hot noodles or something."

" That's right. I'll go with you."

However, there were pupils in front and behind. So the teachers waited until they had led them into the waiting room at the pier. Then they spoke to the men teachers and left unobstrusively one after the other. They turned off the street at once into a back alley in order not to attract the pupils' attention. The alley was bordered by rows of souvenir shops and restaurants. Each of them had low eaves from which hung a big lantern. On the lanterns were written in heavy letters: " Noodles," " Sushi," " Saké," " Sea Food," and so forth. Passing by a restaurant the small ceiling of which was decorated with articficial maple leaves suitable for the season, Miss Tamura asked, " Mrs. Oishi, have you heard of a medicine for colds sold at noodle restaurants? How about trying it?"

Just as Mrs. Oishi was about to say "Yes," she was taken aback by the lively and penetrating voice of a young girl who shouted "One tempura!" It was such a heart-rending cry that she almost exclaimed in surprise. It had come out of the restaurant with a rope curtain hanging at the front, a rarity in the locality. Involuntarily Mrs. Oishi looked in and found a girl with her hair dressed in *momoware* style. She had an artificial maple leaf stuck in her hair, together with a highly decorative yet inexpensive pin. She stood looking innocently toward the street, her hands tucked up in her apron. Mrs. Oishi fixed her eyes on her. The girl apparently took the teachers for customers and shouted "Good evening!" in that same penetrating voice. It was the kind of shout uttered by a girl who already took her job for granted. Her Japanese style coiffure and the adult way of wearing her kimono had given her a different look, but her long eyelashes could not deceive Mrs. Oishi's eyes.

"Matsue! Aren't you Matchan?"

The girl was so surprised to be spoken to by an entering customer that she held her breath and stepped backward.

"Didn't you go to Osaka? Have you been here all this time, Matchan?"

When Mrs. Oishi peered at her face, Matsue started
sobbing as if she had finally remembered. Putting her
arm around Matsue in spite of herself, the teacher was
leading her out through the rope curtain, when the
proprietress darted out from the back, with a hasty
clattering of wooden clogs.

"Who are you? I don't want you to take her out
without letting me know," she said in a suspicious
tone. That finally made Matsue talk. To clear away
the woman's suspicion, she whispered to her, "It's
Mrs. Oishi, Mother."

As it turned out, the teachers had no time to eat
noodles.

7

Fledging

From the time of the excursion on, Mrs. Oishi was not very well. She had been absent from school on account of sickness for nearly twenty days, when one morning, soon after the third term began, she received a post card. It read:

Dear Mrs. Oishi,

How are you? Every day, at morning assembly, I think of you and worry about you. Kotsuru and Fujiko say they don't feel like studying without you. The boys say so too. Please get well soon and come back to school. All the pupils from the cape are anxious about you.

Farewell,

SANAE

The letter revealed the true feelings of the cape children. Unexpectedly tears came into her eyes, but the last word made her burst into laughter.

"Look, Mother. This closing seems to be popular these days," she said, showing the letter to her mother, who had just brought in her breakfast.

"Her handwriting's pretty good for a sixth grader, isn't it?"

"Yes, she's at the top of her class. I think she's going to teachers' school eventually, but she's a little quiet. I wonder if she'll make a good teacher, being the way she is," Mrs. Oishi spoke anxiously about Sanae, the girl who usually did not express herself aloud.

"But you used to be a quiet and unsociable child yourself until the sixth grade or so. Look how you've changed! You seem to be quite talkative these days."

"Do I? Do I talk that much?"

"You can't be a teacher if you mind talking, you know."

"That's true. That's why I wonder if Sanae could speak in front of a class."

"Think of yourself. You didn't even have the nerve to sing in front of other people, do you remember? Still you're doing pretty well as a teacher."

"Uh-huh, I used to be that way. The way I like singing now may be a reaction to my childhood."

"Being an only child may have had something to do with your shyness. Is that girl an only child too?"

"No, she's in the middle of about six children. Her big sister is a Red Cross nurse, I hear. Once Sanae wrote in a composition that she'd like to be a teacher. When I ask her a question, she usually doesn't answer. But when she writes compositions, she writes like an adult. That time, she wrote : ' From now on, women should have occupations. Otherwise they will suffer like my mother.' Her mother seems to be having a very hard time."

" That girl's quite like you."

" But, in my case, from my childhood I told everybody that I wanted to be a teacher. But Sanae doesn't say a word. She usually hides behind the others, but she writes extremely well."

" There are various types, you know. I don't think she's particularly reserved, though, judging from this post card."

" Maybe you're right. And this business of ' Farewell.' It's so funny."

Sanae's post card having caused a lively conversation, Mrs. Oishi ate more than usual for breakfast before she knew it. After the meal, she gazed at the card again as if she were looking into a mirror, and soon thoughts of her pupils flashed across her mind one after another.

First she wondered how Matsue was getting along, that girl in a Japanese coiffure who had shouted " One tempura ! " in a piercing voice. Mrs. Oishi had remembered the name of the restaurant near the pier as being " Shimaya," and had written her a letter after

returning home. But no reply had come. Perhaps
Matsue did not know how to write a letter because she
had only had four years of school. Or maybe she
had not received the letter to begin with.

That evening when they were in Takamatsu, the
proprietress, suspicious at first, became so hospitable
when she had learned who they were.

" Is that right! I'm so glad you came. Please have
a seat."

She showed the teachers in and offered them small
cushions on a narrow matted bench. However, it
was only the proprietress who talked, and Matsue
merely stood quietly. When Mrs. Oishi noticed several of her boy pupils gathering in front of the
restaurant and peering through the rope curtain, she
had to stand up and leave.

" I'll see you again. I'm afraid our boat is coming
pretty soon." Mrs. Oishi said good-by, but Matsue
did not follow to see her off. Perhaps she was not
allowed to do so. Mrs. Oishi walked off quickly,
deliberately refraining from a backward glance. The
pupils, following close behind, questioned her, each
in his own way.

" Who's that girl, Mrs. Oishi? "

" Are they your relatives? "

None of these boys were from the cape, and probably for that reason, they had not recognized Matsue,

who had been to the main school only once. Mrs. Oishi was glad for Matsue's sake that she had had enough presence of mind not to bring the girl out into the street.

Even today Mrs. Oishi could not think of Matsue without a certain frustration. Her pupils had all been born in the same year, had been brought up in the same locality, and had entered the same school. But within such a narrow circle, wide gaps had already formed in regard to their circumstances. What kind of future would be awaiting Matsue, who had been thrown into a strange, unpredictable environment because of her mother's death? Her friends who had started life with her were already preparing for the future in their own ways. When Mrs. Oishi told them to write what they would like to be, Sanae had written " educator." The fact that she had used this particular expression instead of " teacher," as ordinary children would have done, showed that it was not a mere dream but a serous resolution. Now in their sixth year of school the pupils were beginning to try their tender angels' wings with all their might.

Masuno had the most unique ambition. Once at the school recital, she had sung " The Moon over the Ruined Castle " to the admiration of the whole school. She sang whenever she had time and improved more and more. In the matter of singing, her brains were capable of functioning especially well, and she sang all by herself, reading the music, which was quite a rare accomplishment for a country child. Her ultimate dream was to enter a music school, and for that purpose she wanted to go to high school first.

Misako, too, was expected to go to high school. She did rather poorly in her studies and looked depressed, studying overtime after school for the entrance examination. She lacked the ability to comprehend or memorize the fundamentals of arithmetic. However, she was quite aware of this and would have preferred to go to a sewing school which did not give any entrance examination. But her mother would not hear of it. As a result, the poor girl looked gloomier every day. Her mother, wishing to send Misako to the prefectural high school at all costs, visited the school quite often. Apparently she believed that her own enthusiasm could improve her daughter's aptitude. But the girl herself refused to cooperate. She had once said, " I get a headache just looking at figures. How could I take the exam? When the day comes, I'll be sick, I'm telling you." She foresaw her failure because of her poor ability in arithmetic.

In that respect, Kotoe was just the opposite. Although no one helped her at home, she had a special talent for figures just as Masuno had for music. She always received perfect marks in arithmetic. In other subjects, too, she was next to Sanae in marks. She could have entered high school without difficulty, but she said she was not going beyond the sixth grade. Whether or not she was resigned to her lot, she did not seem to be envious of the others. Mrs. Oishi had asked once, " Are you determined to quit school after this year? "

Kotoe nodded.

" You like school, though, don't you? "

Kotoe nodded again.

" Take the upper grade school course for a year then, if not longer."

The girl remained silent, with her head down.

" Shall I talk to your parents about it? "

Then Kotoe spoke for the first time. " But everything is settled now. I made a promise," she said with a lonesome smile.

" What kind of promise? To whom did you give your word? "

" To Mother. She let me go on the excursion because I promised to quit school at the end of this year."

" Isn't that a shame! Can't you break your promise even if I ask her? "

Kotoe shook her head and muttered, " No, I can't." Then she forced a smile, showing her front teeth. " My sister Toshie is coming to the main school next year. If I took the upper grade school course here, there would be no one to cook supper. I'll have to do the cooking next time."

" My! Toshie is only a fourth grader, and she's cooking now? "

" Yes."

" Does your mother still go fishing every day? "

" Yes, almost every day."

The teacher remembered that Kotoe had once written in a composition: " I am sorry to have been born a girl. My father always complains about my not being a boy. Because I am not a boy and cannot go fishing with my father, my mother goes with him. In my place, she goes out to the sea to work, on cold winter days and on hot summer days. When I grow up, I will do whatever I can for her."

That was it, Mrs. Oishi thought. Kotoe seemed to consider it her own fault that she had been born a girl. That was what had made her so reserved about everything. It was too late to question who had put that thought in her head. The girl had already accepted the fact that this was to be her last school year, as if it were her fate.

" But, Kotoe, . . . " Mrs. Oishi meant to say that Kotoe was in the wrong, but stopped. She thought of saying " How admirable of you! " but refrained from it, too. She was not able to say " I deeply sympathize," either.

"I'm sorry to hear that," she finally said—a suitable expression that seemed to comfort and cheer up the girl. Kotoe answered, showing her large, slightly protruding front teeth even more: "But I have got something to look forward to. Two years from now, when Toshie is through with the sixth grade, Mother will send me to a seamstress's. And when I become sixteen, I'll go into service in Osaka. I'll spend all my salary on kimonos. That's what my mother did."

"And then you'll get married, won't you?"

Kotoe smiled a little bashfully. Apparently she had made up her mind to submit to her fate as something unchangeable. She seemed ready to accept meekly whatever awaited her. When she became eighteen or nineteen, she would be called back from her master's house by a fake telegram that would read: "MOTHER SERIOUSLY ILL." On her return, she would be married by her mother's arrangement to a hard-working farmer or fisherman.

Kotoe's mother had married that way and had given birth to six children. Because five of them were girls, she felt constrained in her husband's presence, as if she alone were to blame for if. Affected by this attitude, Kotoe had become as reserved as her mother. The latter went out to sea with her husband every day; her face was tanned like a fisherman's, and her hair, exposed to the sea breeze, had discolored and become rough. For all that, she was going to make her daughter follow the same steps as if she had no regrets. Kotoe, too, took it for the normal life of a woman. Conservative and old-fashioned, they both could have been compared to stagnant water that knows nothing of a clear stream.

Mrs. Oishi was irritated as she wondered if that was the limit of satisfaction for an honest yet poor fisherman's family like Kotoe's. All she could do, however, was to sigh, for she knew that sending Kotoe to the upper grade school would not change the way of thinking of the girl's family.

As she wondered now what an ideal teacher-pupil relation should be, she thought of Mr. Inagawa, editor of *The Seeds of Grass*. Mr. Inagawa, who had been labeled "traitor" and imprisoned, occasionally sent closely written letters from prison to his pupils. They were normal letters, no different from what ordinary people would write, and yet it was said that they were not read to his class. "Was this the way things must go?" she asked herself. Teachers could only afford to contact their pupils superficially, in classrooms and through authorized textbooks, and they had to realize that they would be unwittingly trapped unless they kept their pupils at a certain distance, even if the latter wished to get closer. Unconsciously everyone had become used to prying out others' secrets with his eyes and ears.

At the same time Mrs. Oishi had to watch out sometimes to avoid unexpected tricks. When she told her class she would be staying away from school for some time because of illness, Kotsuru had asked pryingly. " Is it morning sickness? "

Involuntarily the teacher blushed, and some of the pupils jeered. She resented Kotsuru's forwardness but replied frankly: " Yes, I'm awfully sorry. I've lost a lot of weight because I can't eat anything. I'll come back when I get better."

It was since then that she had been absent from school. Now she remembered that it was also Sanae who had looked most worried when she had announced her intended absence. Mrs. Oishi took out the photograph taken six years ago. She had had thirteen copies printed but had somehow neglected to distribute them to the children, and they were still in a paper bag inserted in her album. Among all the innocent-looking children, Kotsuru looked most mature, as might be expected.

Kotsuru had always been by far the tallest of all, and today she appeared about two years older than the others. While the other girls wore their hair either in a Dutch cut or parted on the side, she alone wore her front hair down in a Chinese girl's fashion, assuming the airs of a grown-up. After Masuno had left the cape village, Kotsuru seemed to have become the only boss. She was going to a school for mid-wives after completing the upper grade school. That might have been the reason why the precocious girl had thought of morning sickness.

Fujiko, another girl from the cape, was the only one whose future course had not yet been determined. It was said that her family's property would finally pass into other hands. Mrs. Oishi suspected that maybe that was the reason why poor Fujiko was unable to determine her course despite her approaching graduation. She felt sorry for the girl who, like Kotoe, was awaiting the future submissively. Fujiko was a thin girl with a pale, sallow face. She always seemed to be shivering, her hands in her sleeves, her dignity barely surviving in her cold, gloomy eyes and in her quietness.

The boys, on the other hand, were quite lively.

"I'm going to high school," Takeichi had once announced proudly.

Tadashi said equally proudly, "I'll take the upper grade school course here. After I graduate, I'll do fishing until I'm drafted. Once I'm drafted, I'll work my way up to be an N.C.O. I'll be a sergeant or something, so you remember that."

" My, an N.C.O. ! " Mrs. Oishi exclaimed, but no one detected what was going on in her mind. It seemed strange to her that Tadashi, who had once tried to show the difference between crabs of moonlit nights and those of moonless nights by really bringing live specimens, should have wished to be an N.C.O. But for him there was a good reason. His oldest brother had spent three years of active service in Korea and then, instead of being discharged, he had been sent to the battle front to participate in the Manchurian incident. Recently he had returned home as a corporal. That had stirred up the boy quite a bit.

" If you're determined to be an N.C.O., you can easily go up to the rank of a sergeant, I hear. N.C.O.'s get monthly salaries, too." Tadashi spoke for the course of life he had chosen.

Takeichi retorted loudly : " I'm going to be a cadet. You can't beat me, Tanko. I'll be a second lieutenant right away."

Kichiji and Isokichi looked envious. Unlike Takeichi and Tadashi, they belonged to families that lived from hand to mouth. There was no guessing how they might talk with their families about war, and yet it was certain that they would be drafted eventually like the others, whether or not it was their wish. In the previous spring (1933) Japan had withdrawn from the League of Nations, cutting herself off from international society. But what significance it had, and also in what way it was related to the imprisonment of a teacher of a nearby school, were utterly unknown to the boys. They did not even know that they were deprived of the freedom to be informed of all these things. On the contrary, the warlike atmosphere that had spread all over the country had influenced them so much that they were dreaming of becoming patriotic heroes.

"Why do you want to be a soldier so much?" Mrs. Oishi asked Tadashi. His answer was frank: "Because I'm not the heir. Besides, it's much better to be an N.C.O. than to be a fisherman."

"Hm. . . . And you, Takeichi?"

"I'm the heir, but I'd rather be a military man than a rice dealer, too."

"I see. But I wonder. You'd better think it over anyway." She felt restrained from speaking further and had looked at the boys without another word.

Tadashi, apparently having sensed something, asked, "Don't you like soldiers?"

"No, I like fishermen and rice dealers better."

"Do you? Why?"

"You're still too young to die, you know."

"What a scaredy cat!"

"Yes, that's what I am."

Even now she felt depressed, as she recalled how the vice-principal had warned her just because she had talked that much with the boys. " Mrs. Oishi," he had said. " You're spoken of as a Red. You'd better watch out."

" What in the world is a Red? Why do they call me a Red when I don't know anything about Communism? "

Mrs. Oishi, who was lying in bed, thinking about various things, called to her mother in the dining room. " Mother! "

" Yes? " answered her mother through the sliding doors. She did not come in but remained sitting by the brazier, busying herself with sewing.

" I've got something to talk over with you. Will you come here? "

The daughter heard footsteps and then saw the sliding door opened by a hand wearing a thimble. " I'm awfully sick of teaching. What would you say to my quitting this coming March? "

" Quitting? How come? "

" Opening a cheap candy store or something would be better than teaching. I'm sick of jingoistic school education."

" Hush! "

" Why on earth did you make me into a teacher? "

" Are you blaming it on me? Wasn't it your own choice? You said you didn't want to be as miserable as I, didn't you? It's really no fun sewing kimonos for other people at this age."

" You're better off than I, though. Look at me. I've been teaching my pupils from the first grade on, but now more than one half of the boys want to be soldiers. What's the sense of teaching, I wonder? "

" They're just swimming with the current, you know. You can't end the war by becoming a candy dealer, can you? "

" Oh, I'm sick and tired of the whole business. What's worse, I was senseless enough to marry a sailor. I should have learned a lesson from your past. These air drills these days really take ten years off my life. Even if the ocean is calm, just one bomb hitting my husband's ship could make a widow out of me. I wonder if I should tell him so and ask him to change his job before it's too late. I don't mind helping him do farming or anything else. I'm going to have a baby, and I don't want my child to be fatherless as I was. You wouldn't object to his quitting, would you? "

" You blame everything on me, don't you? Didn't you choose your own husband? I was the one who wanted to object that time. I thought it would be awful if you had to repeat my life. But I accepted whatever you said because you were fond of him. Now it's too late to talk that way."

" I didn't love him because he was a sailor. Anyway, I don't want to teach any more."

" Do as you please. Your nerves are on edge now, I know."

" No, they aren't."

Mrs. Oishi talked quite differently from the way she did at school. But behind her capricious way of talking was her great love of human life.

Before long she got well enough to go back to school. Then the new school year began, and it was already time for her to say good-by. Some of the colleagues were sorry to see her leave; some others envied her. However, no one tried to detain her, because, somehow or other, she had become conspicuous and a subject of discussion. Strangely, no one could say exactly in what respect she was to be criticized. Of course, Mrs. Oishi did not know either. Perhaps the devotion of her pupils to her might have been undesirable.

On the last morning, Mrs. Oishi stood in front of all the pupils of her school—seven hundred in number. For a while, she looked around at them silently. Her eyes gradually dimmed with tears, till at last she caught sight of the tall Nita, who stood at the rear of the group of new sixth graders, gazing intently in her direction. Her eyes filled, and she could not say the words of farewell she had prepared. After bowing in Nita's direction as if he were the representative of the pupils, she got down off the platform. Only then she saw, among the seventh graders, Tadashi, Kichiji, Kotsuru, and Sanae fixing tearful eyes on her.

When, during the noon recess, she visited the detached classroom of the seventh grade girls, Kotsuru caught sight of her immediately and came up running.

"Why did you quit, Mrs. Oishi?" asked Kotsuru in a tearful voice, which was quite unlike her. Behind her, Sanae's moist eyes glistened.

Masuno, who had been loudest in anticipation of high school, had, after all, stayed in primary school to take the upper grade course. But she was not here today. As usual, Kotsuru explained it exaggeratingly: "Masuno's grandmother and father objected to her going to high school so much she finally gave up. They told her it would be all right for a restaurant proprietor's daughter to play the samisen, but they didn't like her to be a concert singer. She cried desperately, not even eating her meals. . . . Another thing, Mrs. Oishi. Misako's school isn't a high school. It's a very small school called the Green School. There are only about thirty students, and it's only a little bigger than a dressmaker's shop.

She'd better have taken the upper grade school course here with us, don't you think?"

Mrs. Oishi laughed. After that she reproved the girl. " You shouldn't talk that way, Kotsuru. Now tell me something. Why is Masuno absent?"

" She's so ashamed of herself she stays away."

" Comfort her and tell her she needn't be ashamed, will you, Kotsuru and Sanae? And how's Fujiko?"

" You'd be surprised, Mrs. Oishi. It's an amazing story," answered Kotsuru loudly and raised her brows in a fruitless effort to open her narrow eyes wide. " She moved to Hyogo Prefecture with her family. During the spring vacation, Dad gave them a ride and carried the whole family of five and their baggage in his boat. The baggage consisted of mats, quilts, pots and pans—that was all. They had only one bureau. It was so old its paint was worn off. The rest were wicker trunks. Fujiko's family hasn't done any hard labor yet, so people were anxious and said that they hoped they wouldn't become beggars or something. They also said that they hoped Fujiko wouldn't be sold to a geisha house or some place like that. . . . " Kotsuru went on to say that Fujiko's family had paid their passage half in cash, half with the rest of the furniture left unsold. Mrs. Oishi patted her on the shoulder. " Kotsuru, aren't you a little too talkative? You're going to be a midwife, aren't you? A good midwife doesn't talk about other people very much, I'm sure. This is my last word for you. Please be a good midwife, will you?"

Brash as she was, Kotsuru shrugged her shoulders with embarrassment and smiled with her narrow eyes. "I understand. Thank you."

"And Sanae, I hope you'll make a good teacher. I think you'd better be a little more talkative, though. That's my last word for you." Mrs. Oishi patted Sanae on the shoulder, and the girl nodded and smiled without speaking.

"If you see Kotoe, give my best to her. Tell her that my last word for her was: 'Take care of yourself and become a good bride some day.'"

Kotsuru talked back promply: "Please be a good mother. That's my last word for you." She patted the teacher on the shoulder playfully. She had grown almost as tall as Mrs. Oishi by now.

"Thank you," said Mrs. Oishi and laughed heartily.

The boys and the girls had been separated from each other into different rooms when they moved up to the seventh grade, so Tadashi and the other cape village boys were not there. Feeling reluctant to go to the boys' classroom and take leave of the cape boys in particular, Mrs. Oishi decided to go right home.

"Give my best to Tanko, Sonki, and Kitchin. Tell them to come and see me when they feel like it."

" How about us girls, Mrs. Oishi? " Kotsuru put in.

" Of course you're welcome any time. You come anyway without my telling you, don't you? You did that long ago. Oh, that reminds me." Mrs. Oishi took out the pictures and gave one to each of the girls. Kotsuru laughed raucously, dancing with excitement.

The next afternoon, Mrs. Oishi was taking a nap, lonely and distracted as though she had had a treasure stolen, rather than glad about being free from work, when Takeichi and Isokichi showed up together unexpectedly. Surprised at the too quick effect of her message, she received the boys without even fixing her disorderly hair.

" I'm so glad to see you. Come right in."

The boys looked at each other. Then Takeichi said, " We're taking the next bus back. It leaves in ten or fifteen minutes, so we don't have time to come in."

" Oh, really? How about taking the bus after that? "

" That would reach the cape after dark," replied Isokichi resolutely. The boys seemed to have made up their minds about this on their way.

" I see. Wait a second then. I'll see you to the bus stop. Let's talk as we walk, shall we? "

Fixing her hair hurriedly, she asked, " When does high school begin, Takeichi? "

"Day after tomorrow."

Takeichi already showed the airs of a high school student, new cap in hand. Isokichi, too, had an unfamiliar-looking hunting cap in his right hand and held his striped, home-spun kimono modestly at the knee.

"Didn't you go to school yesterday, Isokichi?"

"No, I'm not going to school any more," answered Isokichi. He suddenly became rigid and bowed low. "You have been so nice to me all these years. I must say good-by now."

"Oh, not yet. I'm coming with you." Mrs. Oishi smiled, suppressing her tears, and started with the boys. It was a six-minute walk to the bus stop. She walked between the two boys. Isokichi looked up from under the big cap that completely covered his head.

"I'm leaving for Osaka tomorrow night to be an apprentice. My master will send me to night school there."

"Oh, dear! I didn't know that at all. Was it arranged all of a sudden?"

"Yes, Mrs. Oishi."

"What trade?"

"It's a pawn shop."

"My! Are you going to be a pawn shop keeper?"

"No, just a head clerk. I was told I could be a

head clerk if I worked there until I got drafted."

Isokichi had been stiff, using formal language. To make him relax, Mrs. Oishi said, "Be a good head clerk, Isokichi. Please write me every once in a while. Did you receive the picture I sent by Kotsuru yesterday? I want you to cherish the memory of that day."

The boys both laughed.

" This is my farewell present for you, Isokichi. It's post cards and stamps." She handed him a package of a book of postage stamps, post cards, both of which she had been given by someone, and a new towel. To Takeichi she gave a gift of two notebooks and a dozen pencils.

" When you come home for holidays, be sure to look me up, will you? I want to see you grow. You were the first and the last pupils I taught, you know. Let's always be good friends, shall we? "

" Yes," answered Isokichi alone.

" And you too, Takeichi."

" Yes."

When the bus appeared at the bend at the edge of the village, Isokichi took off his cap again and said, " You have been so nice to me all these years. I must say good-by now."

He parroted it stiffly, and then quickly put on his cap. The cap, big enough for an adult, gave him the appearance of a child in the comics, and yet it was becoming. Isokichi, with his hunting cap on, and Takeichi, with his school cap on, waved their hands at the rear window of the bus. Mrs. Oishi gazed after them until they were out of sight. Then she went slowly down to the beach. Across the calm bay lay the long cape village as usual. She thought of the children, growing, trying their wings.

"You have been so nice to me all these years. I must say good-by now," she muttered as though speaking to the cape. It was an expression that sounded funny, sad, and warm at the same time, and perhaps implied more.

8

Yellow Roses

Although it was already March, there was still a chill, as sharp as a razor's edge, lurking in the morning air. Staying in the shade made one shiver from the feet up.

At the bus stop in K- Town, two passengers were waiting for the bus—an old man perhaps a little over sixty, and a woman about thirty. Appartently they had already finished their business in town in spite of this early hour.

" My, it's cold ! " grumbled the old man.

" Isn't it ! " agreed the woman, although he had not addressed her.

As the cold probably had the effect of making human hearts closer to one another, these two persons were talking in a friendly manner before they knew it.

" The cold weather is lasting pretty long this year."

" It really is. With spring just around the corner."

Holding a square package to her chest, the woman sent an interested look toward a plain knapsack which hung unwrapped from the old man's arm.

" Is that for your grandchild ? "

"Yes, it is."

"I bought one for my son too," she said, looking at her package. "I heard they were going on sale to-day, so I took the first bus over. But I couldn't find any good knapsacks like the ones we used to have. These cardboard ones won't last more than a year."

The man nodded in agreement. "There are lots of good ones on the black market, I hear." He laughed, opening his mouth wide. Its inside looked dark, with the back-teeth missing.

The woman said, looking away: "They sell any-thing on the black market these days, even knapsacks for schoolchildren. Isn't it annoying?"

"You can buy anything if you only have money. There are lots and lots of sweets and cakes of all sorts in some places, I hear." With that, a drop of saliva almost fell from the corner of his toothless mouth. He really must have had a weakness for sweets. He wiped his lips with his palm and, as if to conceal his em-barrassment, pointed across the street with his chin.

"Let's wait on the other side, Aunty. The sunshine is the only thing that's free," he said and crossed the street quickly toward the opposite bus stop. Grinning at the word "Aunty," the woman followed him. "'Aunty'!" she repeated the word in her mind and looked up at the tall man. She asked him, smiling, "Where do you live, Grandpa?"

" Me? I live near the Big Rock."

" Do you? I live by the Pine Tree."

" Oh, I see. I used to have a friend there. We were both sailors at one time. His name was Kakichi Oishi, but he died long ago. I guess you don't remember him."

It made the woman start. " Good Heavens! He was my own father!"

This time it was the man who was taken aback. " Isn't that a coincidence! I'll be darned! To meet Kakichi's daughter after so many years! Come to think of it, you really remind me of him."

" Do I really? My father died when I was only three, so I don't remember anything about him. How long ago were you friends with him, Uncle?" She changed " Grandpa " to " Uncle," thinking that her father would be about that age if he were alive.

This woman was, of course, Mrs. Oishi—eight years after we had seen her last. During all the years she had spent as a sailor's wife, the world had been undergoing a far more violent change than when she had angrily quit her teaching job. The China incident had occurred; the Anti-Comintern Pact between Japan, Gemany and Italy had been concluded. The movement called " Mobilization of the National Spirit " had been carried out, teaching the people not to discuss politics even in their sleep, but to look the war in the

face, to believe in the cause, and to put their hearts
and souls into it. They had been forced to do so.
It had become impossible for them to get through life
unless they concealed and tried to ignore their own
dissatisfaction.

It was under such circumstances that Mrs. Oishi had
become the mother of three children. Daikichi and
Namiki, the two oldest were boys; Yatsu, the young-
est, was a girl. It was because she had come to look
very much like any ordinary housewife that she had
been addressed as " Aunty." But a closer observation
of her, especially of her bright eyes, would have revealed that she was not a mere " Aunty."

" Would you mind having tea with me, Uncle? "
she suggested, pointing at the tea house by the bus
stop. She wanted to hear more about her father from
the old man. But he shook his head stubbornly.

" No, thank you. The bus is coming pretty soon.
I guess I'll wait right here," he answered more formally
than before. " And how's Kakichi's bride getting
along? "

" She's very well, thank you," she broke into a
smile, hearing her old mother referred to as " bride."
She would tell her mother about it first thing when
she got home. Just then a bus came from the opposite
direction, honking. She quickly moved away from
the bus stop sign to show that she was not going that

way, but the bus stopped just the same. Standing under the eaves of the tea house, she casually watched the passengers getting off. Only young men got out of the jam-packed bus. They came out of the door in succession; it seemed as though almost all the passengers were getting off here. While looking at them, Mrs. Oishi remembered that a physical examination for conscription was being given at the public hall of that town today. "Oh, that's why," she thought, looking at the youthful faces of the boys one after another.

"Oh, Mrs. Koishi!" There was a shout that was startlingly loud. Almost at the same time, Mrs. Oishi exclaimed just as loudly, "Oh, Nita!"

Looking at the boys coming out one after another, she said, "Oh, my! Oh, my! You're all here. Good Heavens!" Following Nita were Isokichi, Takeichi, Tadashi, and Kichiji—all the cape boys she had once taught.

"Glad to see you again, Mrs. Oishi," Takeichi greeted her first. He was a senior at a university in Tokyo. His face had become thinner, and he seemed to carry the smell of the big town with him. Next, Tadashi bowed with a good-natured smile and scratched behind his ear bashfully. He was working at a shipyard in Kobe and had the strong-willed look of a trained worker. Isokichi stepped forward next, as though he had been waiting his turn. "How have you been,

Mrs. Oishi?" he asked with a sociable smile on his abnormally pale face.

Kichiji, quiet and reserved as ever, only bowed from behind the others, sniffling. He had not left the cape village, but was working as a lumberjack and fisherman there.

Nita was an assistant to his father, a soap manufacturer. In his newly-tailored khaki suit, he looked better off than the other boys. Being as unreserved as ever, he did not stand on ceremony like his friends. "I met Fujiko the other day," he said, and repeated proudly, "I met Fujiko." Mrs. Oishi deliberately ignored him and looked up at each of the boys around her. The passage of eight years had turned the little boys into tall and husky youths.

"So it's already examination day." Tears welled up in her eyes despite herself, blurring the image of the boys. But she realized that this was not the way to behave, and instantly resumed the voice of a former teacher. "Now off you go! Won't you come to see me together some time?"

They left her without reluctance, like the boys that they were. She gazed after them with a variety of thoughts and feelings. Talking like a teacher for the first time in many years had given her a refreshing kind of joy.

She turned around and saw the old man waiting in

the sun by the tea house, avoiding the dust raised by
the bus. In the sunny hedge near by, there was a bush
of yellow roses. It had a great many buds on it, and
they weighted its sprays down. The man broke one
of the sprays nonchalantly. Gazing after the boys
also, he whispered, " Isn't that a shame! Why do
those boys with such big smiles have to be made into
targets for bullets?"

" It's really a shame."

" I can't say this aloud. If I did, I'd be like this."
Still holding the knapsack, he put both his hands behind his back as though they were tied, and went on
to say in a quiet voice : " The Anti-disturbance Law,
you know. I'd be thrown into jail."

He talked like a young man now, as though he had
suddenly recovered his back-teeth. Mrs. Oishi did
not know much about that particular law. It was only
associated in her mind with Mr. Inagawa, editor of
The Seeds of Grass, who, because of a violation against
it, had been imprisoned and, in spite of being released after a short while, had not only been unable
to return to his position but was not receiving just
treatment even now. It was said that his mother stood
up for him almost like an insane woman and was busy
telling whomever she met how her son repented
whatever wrong he had done. There was no telling
to what extent that rumor was true. It was certain,

however, that Mr. Inagawa now lived a solitary life, raising chickens. He had not detached himself from the world; on the contrary, it was the world that cast him out. The eggs he raised were scorned as if they were poisonous, and at one time, he had had no customers at all. The times had taught the people to be submissive, to shut their mouths, to close their eyes, and to stop their ears like the proverbial monkeys. The old man confronting Mrs. Oishi, however, talked to her as if he were inciting her to rebel. " I may be the daughter of his old friend. But after all this is the first time we've ever met. Why then does he take me into his confidence? " She became half-suspicious and tactfully changed the topic.

" Speaking of my father again, when were you friends with him? "

The man smiled, recovering his expression of a toothless old man.

"Well, let me see. We were about seventeen or eighteen then. We were both ambitious. We planned to grab an opportunity to stow away on a foreign ship and sail to America. We thought we would jump into the sea off Seattle or somewhere and swim to the shore."

" My goodness ! I hear there were people who really did that, though."

" Sure. We pretended to be anxious to make money in America, but the fact was that we didn't want to be drafted. We'd be like this today." He put his hands behind his back again and smiled.

" You didn't succeed after all, did you? "

" No, we didn't. But at that time, sailors were exempted from conscription. And in the meantime, both your father and I became fond of sailing, and we decided to be licensed sailors. We worked pretty hard. We hadn't been to school, so it took us five years or so to become second mates. Kakichi passed the exam one year ahead of me. That made me work even harder, and I received my license the next year. But . . . " He went on to say that he had been unable to inform his friend of the good news because Kakichi's ship had been wrecked never to bring him back.

Her father, as described by the old man, sounded different from the image of him her mother, as his wife, had given her. As she pictured her father in his youth, she felt herself smiling instead of feeling sentimental. Perhaps it was due to the affectionate tone in which the old man had talked about him. She was now able to visualize him as a lively and lovable youth. She had heard for the first time, however, that he had disliked being drafted. Had her mother not told her about it because she herself hadn't heard anything from Father? Or had she been another quiet, obedient subject? Mrs. Oishi thought she would ask her about it later when she told her about the business of the "bride." With all these thoughts in mind, she kept on talking with the old man.

"How long have you been sailing?"

"Until about ten years ago. By that time I had become captain of a small ship. I wanted to send my son to navigation school to make a sailor of him without much trouble. But he said he didn't want to be a sailor. So I sent him to commercial school. Later he became a bank clerk, but he was drafted and killed."

"At the front?"

"Yes."

"Oh."

"At Nomonhan. And this is for his son," he said, shaking the knapsack. A sheet of cardboard rattled inside.

Mrs. Oishi almost said, "Having a son is a source of worry," but swallowed the words at the last minute.

There were quite a few passengers in the bus, and the old man and Mrs. Oishi could not sit next to each other. Mrs. Oishi sat down at the rear. With her eyes closed, she thought of her former pupils she had seen just a little while ago. They would be standing in front of the examiners, stripped from head to toe. The number of wooden graveposts in soldiers' cemeteries was increasing steadily, but the youngsters were

expected not to think of them as much as they did of
the tombs of their ancestors. To be more accurate,
they were expected to pay due attention to the war
dead, applaud them, and consider it an honor to follow
them. For what was Takeichi studying, and for
whom was Isokichi going to be a merchant? Did Tadashi, who, as a child, had wished to be an N.C.O.,
associate warships with graveyards? At a critical period
like this, when people ought to conceal what was
behind their smiles, only Nita had seemed carefree,
talking aloud. But who could tell what hidden
thoughts Nita had?

It was certain that those five boys from that small
village, who had reached conscription age this year,
would all be sent to remote places as soldiers. How
many of them would ever come home safely? The
military was the sort of organization that would grant
a week's leave just to increase "human resources."
Women who produced "human resoures" ought not
to worry even if the future of their babies might lead
to wooden grave-posts. Did both men and women
have to submit to their fate? Men, anyway, were
unable to evade their lot. And how about women?

Of the seven girls in Mrs. Oishi's original class,
Misako alone was not having a hard time. After
graduating from the Green School, she had entered a
marriage school in Tokyo. While still in school, she

had gotten married and had had a baby right away. Despite the difficult conditions of the times, she was exceptionally well off, like a person who basks in a sunparlor on a windy winter day.

On the other hand, Masuno, the music lover, had had an extremely hard time. Obsessed with the desire to sing, and rebelling against her parents, she had run away from home several times. Once she had been awarded the first prize in a contest sponsored by a local paper in which she had participated without her parents' knowledge; her performance had been written up in the paper. That was the first time she had ever run away. Every time she disappeared, she had been discovered; and every time she was brought home, she had sneaked off again. Invariably it had been her zeal for singing that had caused her to run away. Why should she not sing—a girl who wanted to sing and was good at it? When she was discovered for the third time, she had been about to make her debut as a geisha. Clinging to her mother who had come for her, she had said, crying: "You said it would be all right for me to play the samisen, didn't you?" Since no one knew when, her enthusiasm for music had found a vent in the samisen. Whether or not her parents approved of her playing the instrument, however, they entirely disapproved of their daughter's becoming a geisha, although they themselves ran a restaurant and had to deal with geishas.

Masuno had married a middle-aged man whom she had gotten to know while she had been away from home, and had finally settled down. As her mother had grown older, Masuno had already taken over the position of the proprietress. When, on rare occasions, Mrs. Oishi happened to meet her on the street, she should cling to her fondly and say, " I always miss you, Mrs. Oishi." She was childlike in her expression of joy even to the point of having tears in her eyes. But her quiet make-up made her look much older than twenty.

What had become of Kotoe, who, unable to go on to the upper grade school course, had gone into service, hoping to get married eventually? Before she had an offer of marriage, she had come home sick with t.b. It was quite some time since Mrs. Oishi had heard that the girl was laid up in the storeroom by herself, all skin and bones.

As to Fujiko, who had also been unable to go up to the upper grade school course, there was an unpleasant rumor. It must have been the prostitute Fujiko that Nita had come across. Mrs. Oishi had guessed the truth from the expression on his face and had deliberately not asked him any questions. However, she had heard before about the girl from Kotsuru. According to Kotsuru, Fujiko had been sold by her parents. She had been sold, like furniture or clothes, to make it possible for her family to buy their daily bread. If Fujiko, who had grown up without doing any work, had for the first time come to know life as it really was, even though by that sordid profession, then perhaps one might even be glad for her. Yet people looked down on her and held her up to ridicule.

Once Matsue, who seemed to have been wiped out of people's minds, and this time Fujiko—why should those girls be laughed at? At least in Mrs. Oishi's heart, they were cherished and loved as ever.

" How are you, Matsue? How are you, Fujiko? How are you really getting along? " she would occasionally talk to them in her mind.

While for Matsue and Fujiko life had been unkind, Kotsuru and Sanae had prospered. Sanae had graduated from teachers' school with an excellent record and had been awarded the honor of staying on to teach. Her eyes shone even brighter now. Because of Mrs. Oishi, Sanae had become good friends with Kotsuru who had graduated also with honors from midwifery school in Osaka. Kotsuru intended to come home after gaining more experience. Whether intentionally or carelessly, she would sometimes write " Mrs. Oishi-Koshi " on the front of the envelope she sent. At any rate, just as Mrs. Oishi's mother had predicted, the talkative Kotsuru had become somewhat reserved, and the quiet Sanae had grown up to be lively. How curious is the process of human growth!

These two girls came to see their former teacher together, at least twice a year—usually once during the summer holidays and again during the New Year season. They always brought the same presents—not the two same things, but invariably Kotsuru would bring millet cakes from Osaka, and Sanae crackers from Takamatsu. Coming to womanhood, Kotsuru was growing fatter and fatter, and her eyes had become as narrow as threads. Her rather strong character was not as obvious because of her eyes. When she smiled, others felt like laughing, too. It was her habit to giggle first and then offer her gift, saying " My present." Once she had said, " I sometimes think it's tactless to bring the same thing over and over again, but when I was a child, I danced for joy whenever people gave me this present. That's why I do it." Sanae had also offered her package of crackers, saying, " They say a fool sticks to one thing."

Daikichi, Mrs. Oishi's oldest child, called them " Present Aunties " and welcomed them. They seldom visited without spending a full day in merriment. As the war dragged on, however, these presents, too, became hard to obtain. Lately Kotsuru had brought some gauze which midwives use, whereas Sanae had brought notebooks and pencils for Daikichi, who had not yet started school.

Today Mrs. Oishi had bought a knapsack for Daikichi, who had finally reached school age. As she was going home now, her heart overflowed with various memories, perhaps affected by her unexpected encounter with her former pupils.

"The Pine Tree! Anyone getting off?" the conductor called. Mrs. Oishi stood up and hurried to the door. Barely having time to salute to the old man, she put her foot on the step, when suddenly she heard Daikichi's voice: "Mummy!" His voice, piercing and pure, chased away all her thoughts.

"Mummy, I've been waiting for you for a long time."

Ordinarily, his clear voice would make his mother break into a smile. But today it sounded a little sad. She smiled anyhow, and the boy spoke half-reprovingly and half-lovingly: "You were so late coming back I felt like crying."

"Really?"

"When I was about to cry, I heard the horn and saw you. I waved my hand, but you didn't look this way."

"Oh! I'm sorry. I was thinking about something else. I almost forgot to get off here and rode past."

"You did? What were you thinking about?"

Without answering, the mother gave him the package. The boy took it as though it were all what he had come for.

"My! Is this the knapsack? It's small."

"No, it isn't. Try it on."

It fitted him. In fact it was a little too big. Daikichi started to run.

"Grandma! The knapsack!" he shouted loudly in the direction of his house, running toward it, as though trying to make up for the slowness of foot with his voice.

From behind, the way the boy ran and swung his shoulders revealed his unconscious but strong desire to grow up. If it were nothing but war once again that was waiting for this lovable boy, what would be the meaning of having, loving, and bringing up children? Why was it forbidden to value human lives and prevent them from being hit by bullets and smashed into pieces? Did " the maintenance of public peace " mean restricting freedom of thought rather than valuing and protecting human lives?

As she saw Daikichi running ahead, it seemed to her that he, too, would have to follow Takeichi, Nita, Tadashi, Kichiji, and all the other youths who had gotten off the same bus and walked toward the public hall. She felt depressed. "If I, whose child has reached school age only this year, feel this way, there must be a lot more mothers suffering," she thought. "It's throwing out the hearts of millions of mothers into a dump to be burned, as though they were rubbish."

> "Soldiers ride on horseback;
> They march, gun on shoulder.
> They march in high spirits.
> I'd love to be one too."

Children were heard singing in the house; they sang out of tune because they tried to sing too loudly. Mrs. Oishi entered and saw her children marching in a circle; Daickichi, knapsack on his back, was leading Namiki and Yatsu. Their grandmother watched them, with sheer joy on her face. Mrs. Oishi said illhumoredly, as if reproaching her: "Oh dear, aren't you all fond of soldiers! Maybe Grandma doesn't understand my feelings, because she hasn't got a son. I don't think this is the way it should be, though."

"Daikichi!" she called sharply. The boy stopped short, looking blank, with his mouth a little open. While Namiki and Yatsu went on singing and running, shouldering a duster and a battledore like guns, the mother hastily hugged Daikichi as if to make up for his astonishment. Although, with the knapsack, he felt inhuman to her touch like a robot, yet he trembled in sudden joy. His mother's caress, rarely given him because he was the eldest child, intoxicated the six-year-old boy with triumphant satisfaction. He smiled and was about to say something, when Namiki and Yatsu spotted them. They rushed over with a cry. Shouting likewise, Mrs. Oishi hugged them all together. " Such wonderful rascals !—How could I ever—let them be killed !" She shook the children to the rhythm of her words. The three children exclaimed in chorus. They were still too young to understand what kind of feeling was hidden behind their mother's words.

Boys of draft age were given physical examinations in spring and, on the basis of the results, were assigned, on the spot, to various branches of the service, like greens and radishes exhibited at county fairs. As the end of the year drew near, they would leave amid cheers for their new posts. It had been that way for a long time. However, as the scale of the war was enlarged day by day, and the state of affairs became serious, such a slow procedure was no longer possible. Being enlisted meant being shipped to the front. The arch of green cedar leaves erected at the pier with the " Farewell and Welcome " signboad on top had discolored. Cheers to send off and welcome soldiers were repeated all the year around, while, at intervals, the ashes of " triumphal soldiers " in white, square boxes returned with the sea breeze through the arch.

The youths passed in numberless processions through these green arches erected all over Japan, and there seemed to be no end of it. The Pacific War broke out in 1941, and more soldiers were sent off with more cheers and hurrahs.

The recruits of that year, such as Nita, Kichiji and Isokichi, left their village long before the war was proclaimed on the eighth of December in the name of the emperor. On the day of their departure, Mrs. Oishi gave them photostatic copies of that dear old picture, in post card size, together with little farewell presents. (The negative had been lost.) The boys were very glad, for they had all lost their pictures, with the exception of Takeichi.

" Take care of yourselves," she said. Then she added in a quiet voice: " Don't die ' honorable deaths.' Come home alive."

Upon hearing this, the boys became as quiet as they had been in those days when the picture was taken. Isokichi was moved to tears which were hardly perceptible; Takeichi looked away, bowing; Kichiji bent his head quietly; Tadashi nodded with a sad smile. Only Nita answered, " All right, Mrs. Oishi. I'll return victoriously." It was a quiet voice for Nita. Especially the word " return " was spoken with apparent scruple. The time had come when soldiers should not think of returning any more. Did Nita really mean what he said? Flattery and ambiguity were foreign to a straightforward young man like him. He must have been as reluctant to lose his life as anybody else. Perhaps he was the one who expressed this most frankly. They said that some time ago, when it was announced he was a grade A selectee, he had exclaimed, without thinking, " Dammit ! " right in front of the examiners. Everyone present had burst out laughing, and the rumor had spread during that d$_r$y. But, strangely enough, Nita had not received even a slap on the cheek. If his prompt exclamation had not sounded offensive to the examiners because it was so eccentric, he was indeed lucky to have been able to express his real feeling. The account of this incident, in which Nita had spoken as much for the others as for himself, had also reached Mrs. Oishi's ears as amusing news.

Did that Nita really think he would return victoriously?

At any rate, more than a half of the next year went by without a word from the boys. The news of the battle of Midway made the villagers on the coast sober with anxiety and resignation. Some mothers secretly paid frequent visits to the shrines to pray for their sons.

Nita and Tadashi were enlisted men in the navy. There had been no word from Nita, the sailor, since his departure—Nita, whose memory would have made people smile, were it not for his peril.

"Where is Nita talking now in that loud but lovable voice of his?" Mrs. Oishi wondered.

Whenever she thought of one of her former pupils, she remembered, at the same time, all the boys she had seen by the bus stop in K- Town; the old man with a mouth that had looked dark inside when he laughed; and the yellow roses by the roadside whose buds swelled in the "free" sunshine on that cold March day. What darkened her heart even more was the thought of her own husband whose ship had been converted into a military transport some time ago and was now sailing no one knew where. The wives and mothers in the country at war were not even permitted to share their anxiety with one another. How stupid that they should be made to endure this misery merely because there were so many others who bore the same wretchedness. If all those who had been deprived of the right to speak on the pretext that they were not the only unhappy ones, spoke up in unison . . . Oh, but how could that be possible? If even one of them expressed her true feeling, her hands would be tied behind her back, as that toothless old man had said.

Those yellow roses in bud by the roadside must have bloomed but the boys . . .

9

Mrs. Crybaby

It was the fourth of April, 1946—the war had ended the previous year, saving the sea, the sky, and the earth from its horrors. Early in the morning, a boat left the Pine Tree village. It made for the cape, carrying a thin, short, elderly woman who wore navy-blue coveralls with small white checks.

The heavy mist hanging over the calm sea gave the cape the appearance of floating as in a dream. After a while, however, its slender shape gradually became clearer as though awakened by the rising sun.

" Oh, it's finally clearing up," said the boy who was sculling the boat; he looked only a little over ten years old. Working the scull with his whole little body, he gazed with his sparkling eyes at the cape village which still lay a long way off. The woman, who had also been gazing at the village, spoke to the boy affectionately.

" This is your first visit to the cape, isn't it, Daikichi? " Her voice sounded younger than she looked.

" Uh-huh, I've never had any reason to go there, you know," the boy replied without turning around.

" That's right. I haven't been there for a long time
either. It's such an isolated place. It's been eighteen
years since I taught there. My, that's almost two dec-
ades ! No wonder I've gotten so old," said the woman.

This was Mrs. Oishi—after so many years ! Today
she was going back to teaching for the first time in
thirteen years, and to the cape village at that. She used
to bicycle to school with such spirit. Had she already
lost that youthfulness ? Perhaps she had. But that
was not the only reason why she was going by boat.
The war had deprived people of bicycles—a daily
necessity. Half a year after the war, it was still impossible to buy a bicycle. This was what had troubled
Mrs. Oishi most when she was reassigned to the cape.
The bus used to run part of the way, but even that had
been discontinued during the war and had not yet
been resumed. There did not seem to be any
other way than to walk the five-mile road which she,
even in her youth, used to cover by bicycle. She
feared she would certainly lose her health that way,
and suggested that the whole family move to the cape.
Daikichi instantly raised an objection and said he
would ride her back and forth by boat every day.
But it would cost a considerable amount of money
to rent a boat.

" What would you do on a rainy day ? " asked the
mother then.

" I'd wear Daddy's raincoat."

" What shall we do on a windy day? "

Daikichi remained silent.

" Oh, never mind. I'll walk when it blows." She quickly offered to help her son who was at a loss for a reply. Tomorrow would take care of itself. The long, hard years, during which time people had been intent on living from day to day, had at least taught them not to yield to minor difficulties, such as bad weather. The war had decreased the size of the Oishi family from six to three, which had made it all the more necessary for the remaining members to survive.

Daikichi had become a sixth grader, and Namiki a fourth grader. The latter had come to the beach today to see his mother off to work for the first time. Remembering that it was about time for him to go to school, Mrs. Oishi looked back toward the Pine Tree. She had not seen the tree from the sea for a long time, but its appearance had not changed since the old days. Outwardly, her village did not seem to have changed at all. Actually, defeat after a long war had brought about great changes there.

" Aren't you tired, Daikichi? I'm afraid you'll get blisters on your hands."

" Maybe, but they'll heal in no time. I don't mind."

" I really appreciate this. Shall we leave a little earlier after tomorrow? "

" Why? "

" It isn't becoming for a teacher's son to be late for school every day. In the meantime, I'll try to get a bicycle."

" Never mind. I won't be scolded when I have a good reason to be late. I'll give you a ride every day." The boy smiled proudly, rocking himself gently back and forth with the scull.

" Aren't you good at sculling! You're really a seaside child. When did you learn it? "

" I just picked it up. Any sixth grader can do this."

" Really? Maybe I'd better learn it, too."

" No. I'll give you a ride always."

" That reminds me. Once there was a boy whose name was Tadashi Morioka. When he was only a first grader, he offered to take me by boat. It was long ago . . . but he was killed in action."

" Oh! Was he your pupil? "

" Yes."

Suddenly tears gathered in Mrs. Oishi's eyes. If he were alive, he would have been quite a man by now, she thought. She remembered the time when she had parted from Tadashi for good—five years ago, at the pier. Her memory's image of him then appeared to her, overlapping the image of his childhood. That had been the last she had seen of him. How many of her former pupils were gone never more to be seen? Her heart sank as she wondered how many would return home now that Japan had lost the terrible war, and how many she would see again.

The last five years had passed like a bad dream. Mrs. Oishi during that time suffered as much as anyone else till at last she had been compelled to go back to teaching at the remote cape village, escorted by her little son. For the first time in her life, she really found it lucky to be qualified for a profession. It had been her former pupil Sanae who had advised her to submit her application. By that time she had become so hard up that she had hardly anything to wear to school. Being in want ages people rapidly, and so Mrs. Oishi, too, looked much older than forty now. She could even have passed for fifty years old.

People lived and died, sacrificing all human rights. They either kept their eyes wide in apprehension or had to hide the tears that streamed from the corners. Every day they felt driven. What was worse, they had become so used to it in time that they fogot to think about it; spiritually as well as physically, they had become completely coarse and wild. Rebelling against that tendency would have meant death. That kind of unrest seemed to last for quite some time, and the people often felt as though the war were not really over.

On the fifteenth of August, 1945 (everyone had already heard of the cruel effects of the A-bomb through word of mouth but had not yet been informed how cruel they really were), Daikichi, a fifth grader then, had been called to school to listen to the emperor's broadcast. After hearing the imperial proclamation of surrender, he had come home down-hearted, bending his head a little, as though he had taken the responsibility of the defeat on his little shoulders.

It was only a little more than half a year since then. Mrs. Oishi was deeply moved to see her brave little son sculling there in front of her eyes. How quickly children adapted themselves to the change of times! Mrs. Oishi knew that Daikichi would be ashamed if she told him now how he had acted that day the previous August. So she just kept her thoughts to herself.

On that day, she had hugged her son with a smile to cheer up the discouraged boy. "What are you so sad about?" she said. "From now on you can really study the way children should. Come now, let's have lunch."

Daikichi used to get excited over meals, but that day he did not even look at the table. "Mother, we lost the war. Didn't you hear the radio?" His voice faltered tearfully.

"I did. The war's over anyway, though. Isn't it a good thing?"

"Even though we lost?"

"That's right. No one will be killed in battle any more, you see. Those who are alive will come back."

"We didn't stick to the motto 'Death and no surrender.'"

"No. Good thing we didn't."

"Don't you cry even though we were beaten?"

"No."

"Are you glad?" Daikichi asked reproachfully.

"Don't be silly, Daikichi. Think of yourself. Daddy was killed, wasn't he? He'll never come back, Daikichi."

The boy was astonished by her violent tone and looked her full in the face as though awakened for the first time. But his mind's eye had not yet fully opened. He wanted to accuse his mother of having suggested to have lunch despite that serious moment. He had not experienced peace. He had heard he had been born on a dark night during an air drill. He had grown up in blackouts, had gotten used to hearing sirens, and had gone to school with a quilted hood even in summer to protect his head in case of an air raid. Having grown up that way, he was unable to understand why his mother had to hate war that much. Every family had sent someone to war, and there were hardly any young men remaining in the village. Daikichi had taken this for granted. The

grounds of all the shrines had been swept clean without
the trace of a fallen leaf. " This is our way of living,"
Daikichi had believed. The only thing he had not
liked had been bitter bread made from acorns he had
picked in the woods.

During the war, several teen-agers in Daikichi's
small village had volunteered for the Juvenile Air
Corps. " Fliers can eat as much *zenzai** as they want."
—such were the words the military used in order
to capture the immature minds of poor youngsters,
and some sons of needy families were coaxed into
joining the Air Corps. Those boys, however, quickly
became heroes that way. The time had come when
people, whether rich or poor, were labeled unpatriotic
unless they devoted themselves to the " cause." The
boys therefore were praised all the more if they gave
up their studies and volunteered for military sevice
without their parents' consent—especially if they were
only sons. Once when, at the junior high school in
town, many boys volunteered, there were three only
sons among them who had not obtained their parents'
approval. It was considered a great honor for the
school, much to the parents' horror. Daikichi, who
was still too little then, said as if lamenting his im-
maturity : " I wish I could go to junior high soon."

---

* Sweetened bean soup.

Then he went on to sing:

> *" Navy officers' coats*
> *All have seven buttons.*
> *Cherry blossoms and anchors*
> *Are marked on all of them. . . . "*

Human lives were compared to cherry blossoms, and children were taught to believe that the only ultimate goal and infinite honor for a youth was to fall in battle. Education went on, at least, with a view to indoctrinating all the boys in Japan with that belief. Even the statues of Kinjiro Ninomiya, symbols of diligence, were removed from school grounds and were contributed as scrap metal with cheers. Temple bells that had been telling time morning and evening and proclaiming emergencies the past hundreds of years were removed from towers to be melted down. In that environment, it was probably natural that boys like Daikichi had come to want to be heroes and to disregard the value of their lives. This was a trend, however, to which Daikichi's mother never conformed.

"Listen, Daikichi," she said then. "I'd like you to be a civilian. One member of our family has already died an ' honorable ' death. Isn't that enough? You don't gain anything by dying. Do you want so much to be killed after I did my best to bring you up? Wouldn't you mind it if I spent the rest of my life, crying?" She said this as if putting a wet towel on Daikichi's feverish forehead, but the boy was so frantic that her mild admonition had no effect. On the contrary, he tried to reason with his mother, saying, "You couldn't have the honor of becoming a fallen soldier's mother otherwise." He seemed to believe that being killed in action was the best way to be faithful to his parents and the emperor. It was therefore impossible for the mother and the son to agree.

"Heavens!" the mother said. "Do you still want to make me a fallen soldier's mother? I've lost my husband already. Isn't that enough?"

The boy, however, was secretly ashamed of her being that way. Being a boy in a militant nation, he naturally wished to save face. He tried his best not to let others know how his mother felt. He himself was somehow concerned about her words and deeds. He remembered what had happened quite a long time before.

At the time, his father had been home on sick leave, but received sailing orders again. Daikichi was the first to get excited, and he raised a clamor with his brother and sister. His mother frowned a little and said in a suppressed voice, "What's the matter with this boy? Is he mad? He doesn't know what it means to me." With that, she gave him a push on the forehead with her finger. Daikichi, losing his balance, almost fell backward, so he sprang at her angrily. When he saw her eyes filled with tears, however, he stopped in embarrassment. His father comforted him, smiling: "Never mind, Daikichi. Young ones like you ought to be full of pep. If you were sentimental, what should I do? You may make as much noise as you like."

But Daikichi did not feel like raising any more clamor. Then his father hugged all the three children together. "Keep healthy and grow up quickly," he said. "You must all grow up and take good care of your mother and grandmother. The war will be over by then."

"It will? How do you know?"

"A sick man like me wouldn't be needed otherwise."

Still the children could not understand what he meant. They only felt proud because their father was going to war like other people. They had been ashamed until then, because all the members of their family had been staying home. Everywhere in Japan family life had been broken up to that extent.

It was a little before the fall of Saipan that the official notice of their father's death reached the family. Even Daikichi could not help crying then. Holding his elbow in against his chest, he wiped his tears with his wrist. His mother hugged him around the shoulders. "Let's not be discouraged, Daikichi. Please

be a man," she said, trying to encourage him and
herself as well. She then went on to tell him in a
quiet voice how badly his father had wanted to stay
home: " He knew he could never come back once he
left. And yet you were all excited and made such a
racket. I was so sorry for him. I felt awful. . . . "

Even then, however, Daikichi wondered why his
mother talked that way. He wished she had said his
father had gone to war in high spirits. He was, of
course, sorry to have lost his father. But, at the same
time, he accepted his fate as a natural outcome, for
there were many other fatherless children around him.
In the neighboring village, for instance, there was a
family which had lost all its four sons; four badges
of honor were stuck side by side on its gate. With
how much respect Daikichi used to look up at them!
He even felt a kind of envy.

Before long, a small, oblong badge, with the words
" Death of Honor " raised upon it, was sent to Daikichi's house, too. His mother emptied out the
envelope into her palm and looked at the badge, together with the two little nails, for a while. Then
she put them all back into the envelope and placed
it in a drawer.

" It won't do us any good nailing this on our gate.
How silly ! " she muttered angrily and started polishing
rice in a beer bottle. The rice was not for the chil-

dren but for their grandmother who was sick in bed and lived on rice gruel. The old woman had fallen down during an air drill and had been laid up ever since with no hope of recovery. The doctor was of the opinion that she had not been taken ill because of her fall, but had fallen because she had been ill already. The village doctor was an old man over eighty whose hair and beard had turned completely white; he was quite reluctant to visit a patient who had no chance of recovery. Unfortunalely there was no other doctor to consult. Mrs. Oishi therefore tried hard to obtain, at least, something good to eat for her mother, but it was not easy. Even by the seaside it was very difficult to buy fish. She went from one place to another, asking for fish and eggs, but she could not get a thing without the humilation of bowing many times. Yet she kept on trying.

One day she found the badge of honor nailed on the front of the gate. Apparently Daikichi had taken it out of the drawer and nailed it up while his mother had been away. The small badge was glittering in the proper place. The " honorable " widow stood there for a while, looking at it—the small sign of " honor " that had been exchanged for a man's life. The badges of honor were increasing shamelessly in number, decorating one gate after another. Perhaps it was the little children who wanted them most.

The fifteenth of August finally arrived. The whole country fell into confusion, as though a muddy current were sweeping over it. If, in the midst of that chaos, children like Daikichi gradually learned to open their eyes, it was nothing to be laughed at. There was absolutely no reason to ridicule them.

Quite a few people made money, taking advantage of the post-war disorder, and soldiers who had outlived the war were coming home day after day. Some soldiers were unable to return home although they were alive; many fathers, husbands, sons, and brothers who were dead would never come back. Their badges of honor which had been decorating the gates all disappeared as though their families thought that would take their guilt away.

Daikichi, from whose house gate the badge had also been removed, had to meet the sudden death of his sister, Yatsu. Only about a year had passed since his grandmother's death. The girl's was the third death in the family in such a short length of time. Daikichi's father had disappeared into the bubbling ocean; his grandmother had grown thinner and thinner from illness till at last she had fallen like a dead tree; Yatsu was gone like a dream that vanished, although she had been well until the day before. Of those three, Yatsu's death grieved the family most. She had eaten unripe persimons in secret and had died of acute intestinal catarrh. The persimons would have been ripe in a month or so, but she had not waited but eaten some because they were not astringent. Some other children had eaten persimons with her, but only Yatsu had died.

"The war's over, but Yatsu was killed because of the war just the same." When his mother said that, Daikichi was unable to see her meaning right away. He gradually understood, however, what she meant. Lately persimons and chestnuts did not stay on the trees in the village until they ripened, for no one was patient enough to wait. Children would always go out into the fields and eat any kind of weed that was edible. They would eat dirty sweet potatoes raw. They all had bad complexions, probably from round-worms. But there was no doctor for the villagers who might fall ill; nor was there any good medicine. Doctors and medicine had all been requisitioned for the war. When the grandmother died, even the village priest had been away on active service. The priest in the neighboring village had been too busy taking care of the war dead. The village priest had returned a little before the end of the war and immediately visited the Oishis' to hold a memorial service for the grandmother's soul. The family had not expected then that they would soon have to ask him again to say a mass for Yatsu.

The grandmother had lamented the village doctor's absence, before her death. But poor little Yatsu, Daikichi imagined, probably had not thought of anything of that sort. He even felt resentful toward the priest who was reciting the sutra loudly. According to Mother, when Yatsu was born, Father had already been feeling sick and had been thinking of quitting his sailor's job in order to recuperate. Father, who had been sailing over the seven seas of the world for many years, had finally wished to come home and rest; he had compared his home to the port on an eighth sea and had named the new-born baby "Yatsu," or the eighth port. Sick as he was, however, Father had been unable to stay home to recover. And now, Yatsu, on whom he had set his hope, had also died.

Everything was in short supply, and Mrs. Oishi was unable to have a coffin made for Yatsu without offering the material. She decided to give away an old bureau which was falling apart. Flowers too had been excluded from the gardens, so Daikichi and Namiki picked some wild flowers in the cemetery to offer to their dead sister.

Long ago, many flowers used to be grown in their garden, the boys heard. But as far back as their memory went, there had been only radishes and pumpkins raised there. Pumpkins were grown even in the small piece of ground under the eaves, and the

vines were climbing up to the roof. Right after
Yatsu's death, her mother, crying, pulled the vines
off the eaves. Three or four untasty-looking pumpkins
came falling down with the vines. She put the best-
shaped one on a tray and offered it on the altar. The
rumor had spread that the girl had died of children's
dysentery, so the family had to keep wake all by themselves by the death bed. That evening, when the
usual power stoppage time was over, the mother
picked up a Solingen knife as though she had suddenly
remembered something, and thrust it right into the
side of the pumpkin, much to her sons' surprise. It
was the knife their father had brought home. The
children had been told many times how sharp and
dangerous it was. If their mother had not been
smiling, they might have screamed in fear. But she
was smiling. Although she looked like a stranger,
with her eyes swollen from crying, the boys were instantly relieved to see by her expression that there was
nothing to worry about.

" Let's make something nice for Yatsu," the mother
said. " Maybe you don't know what this is going to
be. Poor Yatsu never had a chance to see one. You
think all pumpkins should be eaten, whether or not they
taste good, don't you? When I was a kid, I used to be
given untasty pumpkins to play with. See? This is
a window." She carved a square hole in the side of

the pumpkin. " I'll make a round window on this side," she went on. " It's a little difficult. Will you get me a small dish, Daikichi? I want to draw a circle with it. And get me a tray too. I want to put the pulp on it."

The boys watched her with their eyes wide. It was a lantern that she had made. The windows were covered with paper, and a nail was stuck in the bottom for a candle. With a rationed candle burning inside, the lantern turned out to be just what Yatsu would have liked to see. Daikichi forgot his sorrow for a moment and said, " Mother, you are a real craftsman."

When the small coffin was ready, the lantern was put into it beside the little girl's face. Shells and paper dolls Yatsu used to play with were also put in. Her brothers were suddenly overcome with grief and burst out crying. Wailing, Daikichi thought of his puzzle ring Yatsu had always wanted. Reproaching himself for not having been kind enough to lend it to her, he thought he would give it to her now. He tried to make her hands, folded on her chest, hold the ring, but her cold fingers would not accept it any more. The ring slipped and fell down to the bottom of the coffin. Namiki, also crying, brought his colored paper he had been treasuring and keeping away from Yatsu. He folded the sheets of paper, making them into shapes of birds, footmen and balloons, and put them into the coffin. It was with all these presents that Yatsu left for the other world.

After this, Mrs. Oishi suddenly grew old. Her hair became more grey, and she looked even smaller as she lost weight. When she leaned over, she looked exactly like her deceased mother. Little boy as he was, Daikichi was shocked to see her age so rapidly. He feared something might happen to her next. He had grown mature enough to appreciate the value of human life. "Take good care of your mother," his father's words, now took on substance in meaning.

He would say, "I'll get firewood, Mother," and take Namiki with him to the wood.

"I'll get rations on my way home from school." With this, he also took over the job of going to the far-away ration center.

Namiki, too, offered what help he could. "I'll draw all the water you need, Mother," he would say. Their mother, who was moved to tears even more easily than before, muttered: "Why, both of you became so nice to me all of a sudden."

It was due to Sanae's secret efforts that Mrs. Oishi, who had weakened so much and needed so much care, was able to go back to teaching again. Sanae was a teacher at the main school now.

"She's nearly forty, isn't she? That's about the age when women teachers quit their jobs." The principal showed reluctance at first. Sanae, however, entreated him again and again until finally he agreed on condition that Mrs. Oishi was to teach at the cape school—and that, not as a fully qualified teacher which she had the right to be, but as a temporary teacher whose position was completely at the mercy of the principal. In other words, she might be fired any minute if there was a good substitute. Overcome with sympathy, Sanae informed Mrs. Oishi of it. The eyes of the latter, however, glittered in a strange way.

"That's just what I want. I once promised to go back there, you see. So I've been in debt in a way." She did not mind the bad condition at all, and smiled as though a sudden joy were welling up from the bottom of her heart. Just at that moment, the words she had been forgetting until then came back to her memory with the freshness of a flower ready to open.

"Teacher, come again!"

"Come back when your foot gets well."

"It's a promise."

Did she not know that she was pitied just like the "old" Mrs. Goto who had replaced her at that time? Of course, she did. But, being a widow with two little children, she had to go to the cape gladly like Mrs. Goto.

As she watched the green hills on the cape grow nearer, freshly washed in the night air, she felt herself fresh and young too. In the old days, she had been ahead of times with her Western clothes and bicycle. Now, she had her grizzled hair tied up in a simple fashion, wore coveralls made of her husband's old navy-blue kimono, and was having her little son scull the boat for her. If there was anything that reminded one of her former self, it was her eyes which had suddenly begun to shine, and her young voice.

Her Western clothes and bicycle had once been accused of being modern, but they had started a mode just the same. As a result, there was hardly any woman in the cape village now who did not know how to ride a bicycle. Now that nearly twenty years had passed, however, probably no one remembered any more what she had been like in her youth.

The land seemed to slide toward them, and the boat was quite near the beach already. Just as in the past, village children gathered in crowds, at the sight of Daikichi, who was pushing the boat clumsily with a pole, and the unfamiliar-looking Mrs. Oishi. The teacher knew none of them. The shortage of clothing for the past several years had made the children of that frugal village look even more tattered. Some boys wore pants shredded like seaweed, showing their bare skin. When Mrs. Oishi smiled to the children, they either looked a little scared or remained impassive. But they all showed deep interest as they stepped back.

The way they stared with curiosity had not changed
since the old days. Surrounded by those curious
eyes, Mrs. Oishi jumped off the boat. Even a little
pebble seemed to bring back dear memories of the
past. She felt dizzy, probably from seasickness. As
she started walking slowly, she heard the children
whispering behind her:

"Maybe that's the teacher."

"Shall we bow and see then?"

The teacher grinned despite herself. Three or four
little children ran past her and bobbed their heads,
standing in her way. They did not seem to have
reached school age yet, but probably they were emulat-
ing the new first graders, who had adopted the habit
of bowing as the new school year approached. Returning their greeting, Mrs. Oishi felt tears coming to
her eyes. She was happy, feeling as though the little
children were welcoming her. She wiped her eyes
secretly and smiled. She looked at them carefully this
time but did not find a familiar face. People she met on
the road were strangers too. "The road is just the same
as before, but how much the villagers have changed!"
thought Mrs. Oishi. She did not realize that it was
she herself who had changed more than anyone else.
In the meantime, children kept on passing her by twos
and threes. They ran past, stealing a glance at her.
She purposely looked away from them in order to

hide her eyes almost overflowing with glistening tears.

After waving her hand at Daikichi, who was going home by himself, she went through the school gate. The minute she saw that about 80 per cent of the window panes of the weathered schoolhouse were broken, despair assailed her like a rising tide. Later, however, as she sat by the window in the old classroom as she had in the old days and looked out, her back began to straighten; for, although the schoolhouse was as old as could be, she noticed that the pupils were bringing new things with them. Some brought new white satchels made of sash padding; some used homemade wrapping cloths as bags. The texbooks inside had no covers and were as crude as folded newspapers. Still the children's faces glowed with anticipation. Their expression was the same as that of the cape children in the past. It seemed to the teacher as though what she had experienced eighteen years ago had happened only yesterday. For a while, she was even confused into thinking that there had been no time gap between then and now.

After the simple beginning ceremony, she led the children into the classroom. Prepared as she was, she felt a sudden rush of blood into her face. Nevertheless, she called the roll in an experienced manner. She cautioned the pupils first, telling them in a young, steady voice: "When your name is called, please answer ' Present ' loudly. . . . Mr. Kaku Kawasaki."

" Present."

" Mr. Yoshio Kabe."

" PRESENT."

" Aren't you lively! I'm sure you can all answer clearly. Are you Kotsuru's brother, Yoshio? "

The boy who had just been praised for his loud response nodded " Yes." It was as though he believed that he should not answer with his mouth unless his name was called.

The teacher, however, was still smiling.

" Mr. Bunkichi Okada."

Obviously he was Isokichi's nephew. But, knowing that his father was unkind to Isokichi who had become blind and had been discharged from military service, she passed without bringing up his name.

" Mr. Katsuhiko Yamamoto."

" Present."

" Mr. Goro Morioka."

" Present."

Morioka! Tadashi's face appeared clearly in Mrs. Oishi's memory and vanished.

" Miss Makoto Katagari."

" Present."

" Are you Kotoe's sister? "

Makoto gazed back vacantly. Apparently she did not remember her sister who had died in her infancy.

That made the teacher stop asking about the old days. There was Misako Nishiguchi's daughter, too, whose name was Katsuko. Among the three other girls was Chisato Kawamoto, wearing a new red dress. During the recess, Mrs. Oishi could not refrain from asking her in a casual manner: " Your father is a carpenter, isn't he, Chisato? "

Chisato answered, staring with her black eyes which resembled those of Matsue: " No, the carpenter's my grandpa."

" Oh, I see."

The teacher had read in the school register, however, that the girl's father was the carpenter. " Who's Matsue then? Is she your sister? " she asked again.

" No, she's my mother. She's in Osaka. She sent me this dress."

That gave the teacher a shock. She was relieved to remember that there was neither Nita nor Masuno in her new class. At the same time, she could not help missing them. If Nita had been here, all the family affairs of the ten new pupils would have been disclosed by now. He would have given the teacher the popular name or nick name of each one of them. She thought of Nita, Takeichi, Tadashi, Isokichi, Matsue, Fujiko, and all the others. Her ten new pupils who had come to school for the first time today, showing as much trust in their teacher as her former pupils, gave way in her mind to the twelve children who had once gathered under the Pine Tree. Involuntarily she looked out the window and found the tree standing there just as before. It appeared to be unconscious of her two sons who might be standing by its side gazing at the cape.

Mrs. Oishi went to a corner of the playground stealthily and fixed her face secretly. To that sentimental teacher the pupils had already given a nickname, although she was still unaware of it. After all, there was still a Nita in the cape village. The children were too observant to overlook even the slightest motion of their teacher. Her nickname was " Mrs. Crybaby."

10

One Sunny Day

Although it was already April, there was still a chill
hovering over the beach that afternoon. Mrs. Oishi,
who had been sitting on the sand, stretching out her
legs, stood up and dusted her coveralls at the knees.
A voice called to her from behind. "What are you
doing over here, Mrs. Oishi?" It was Misako Nishiguchi.

"Oh, Misako!"

Wearing a formal sash over her lined silk kimono
which had a gay, flowered pattern, Misako appeared
to be going out somewhere. After the exchange of
formal greetings, she suddenly began talking in an
intimate tone: "I was on my way to school. I wanted
to see you." With that, she bowed again and added:
"By a fortunate coincidence, my daughter, Katsuko,
happens to be in your class. I'm very happy about
it."

Her slow way of talking and her decorum were
reminiscent of her mother in former years. But she
quickly revealed her old self and talked affectionately to the teacher: "When I heard you were coming

to the cape again, I was so glad that I cried.   You were
my teacher and now you're my daughter's.   That sort
of thing doesn't happen very often.   Anyway, I'm
glad you've kept healthy."

"Didn't we all pass through hard times, though?"
Without   answering,   Misako   looked   around.
"Wasn't it around here that you got hurt?"   she
inquired with a look of longing for the past in her
eyes.

"Yes, it was.   How well you remember!"

"I'll never forget it.   I often thought of it and
talked about it with Sanae.   We came to think that
our class must have been made up of the most peculiar
children that ever went to school on the cape.   Do
you remember we once walked all the way to your
place?"   With that, she glanced toward the far-away
Pine Tree.   Just then she noticed Daikichi's boat
approaching, and looked puzzled.   The boat had already come quite near.   Nodding toward it, Mrs.
Oishi explained, smiling.   "That's my son, Misako.
He comes to pick me up this way every day."

On hearing this, Misako exclaimed in surprise:
"Oh, does he?"

"Didn't Misako know that Daikichi has been coming
to pick me up for the last three days?"   Mrs. Oishi
wondered.   Misako seemed to have inherited the ways
of her family which had always been aloof.   Never-

theless, the storm of the times had not neglected to cross the high mud wall around her house, to snatch away her husband and place him among the soldiers who had not yet returned. Standing in front of the teacher now, however, she appeared quite carefree like a young girl, smiling as good-naturedly as before. While the other villagers had nothing to wear except plain coveralls, Misako alone was dressed in good clothes befitting a young wife in a rich family. How had she pulled through these long years of various hardships? Right after the war, there had been a rumor that the storehouse of the Nishiguchi family was piled to the ceiling with stacks of military goods, but this had never been proven. They had said that Misako's family had become rich with those goods. but her face revealed no such guilt.

Misako, standing side by side with the teacher showed real anxiety every time Daikichi's boat rocked. " It's too windy for a little boy, Mrs. Oishi. Oh, look ! I'm scared."

At times, it seemed as if Daikichi's little body, together with the skiff, were going to reel into the sea. Both the little boat and the little boy strove with such spirit that the two women, watching him, found themselves to be straining, too. It was chilly on the beach, but Daikichi must have been all wet with perspiration.

" Don't you ride a bicycle any more? " asked Misako. Mrs. Oishi, however, was too nervous to pay much attention to her question, watching Daikichi being tossed about by the waves and wishing she could haul him in, together with the boat.

Misako went on: " Sculling will be too difficult on rainy or windy days. You can save time by bicycle, too, can't you? "

" Yes, but, Misako, bicycles aren't on the market these days. Even if they were, I don't think I could afford to buy one," answered the teacher, without taking her eyes off the boat. She remembered then that even in the good old days she had bought her bicycle on easy payment terms. Tomiko, the bicycle dealer's daughter, who had helped her had gotten married later and settled down in Tokyo. Since the war, when even post cards had become scarce, Mrs. Oishi had not heard from her again. It was toward the end of the war that she had thought once more of her friend whose husband, too, used to run a bicycle store at Honjo in Tokyo. She had wondered where they might be and how they might be getting along; she had feared that Tomiko's whole family might have been killed in that air raid of the ninth of March. Until then her mind had been so much occupied with the quick succession of changes in her lot that she had hardly thought of other people.

The house in K- Town where Tomiko's father used

to live was still a bicycle store. For some reason, however, the shopkeeper had changed during the war,
and now there was only one old man there, who always
looked shabby and repaired dirty old bicycles. The
man, too, had lost his heir.

"Where in the world can I get a new bicycle?"
Mrs. Oishi wondered. Yet Misako spoke in a matter-
of-fact manner: "If you want to buy a bicycle,
please let me know."

There was no time to ask what she had meant, for
Daikichi's boat suddenly picked up speed and approached the beach. Probably it had come under the
lee of the cape now where the wind did not hinder it.
The boy grinned at his mother but looked away from
Misako indifferently. He poled the boat as usual
until its bow ran up on the sand, and waited for his
mother to get in. Just at that moment, the stranger
addressed him unexpectedly from the side, "Come
now, young man. Get off the boat while I hold it
for you."

When he turned around in surprise, his mother
smiled at him. "Why don't you take a rest, Daikichi?"

The boy shook his head without speaking. The
mother went on: "I have something to talk over
with this lady. Will you wait just a little while?"

Angrily Daikichi jumped off the boat without

answering. When he had tied the hawser around a big stone, his mother called, " Come here, Daikichi."

She wanted to ask Misako about the bicycle in his presence. But, when she sat between Misako, who seemed to have forgotten about the subject, and Daikichi, who gazed out across the sea with his arms around his knee like an adult, she somehow did not feel like talking about bicycles any more. " Whatever means Misako may know, it will certainly involve all our scruples afterwards," thought Mrs. Oishi to herself. After an awkward silence Misako started talking light-heartedly as if to put her at ease. " I talked to Sanae the other day, and we thought of getting our classmates together to have a welcome party for you."

" Oh, I'm glad to hear that. But I wonder if I deserve such a party. Before I came back here, I thought I was as young and energetic as ever. But after I came, I found myself much too sentimental. Every memory makes me cry." As she spoke, she already had tears in her eyes. Wiping them away quickly, she continued in a determined voice : " It's awfully sweet of you, though. How many of your classmates live around here ? "

" Two men and three women. But we mean to invite Kotsuru and Matchan, too."

" You mean Matsue Kawamoto ? "

" Yes. For a long time we had no idea where she

was, but during the war she came back once from
God knows where. She stayed here only a little while
and then went away again. But I understand Masuno
has her address. Matchan had gotten so good-looking
I hardly recognized her." For an instant, her face
assumed a strange look. Mrs. Oishi pretended not
to notice it; at the same time, she recalled what had
happened in her classroom two days ago.

"Your father is a carpenter, isn't he, Chisato?"
she had asked.

"No, the carpenter's my grandfather."

"Is Matsue your sister?"

"No, she's my mother. She's in Osaka. She sent
me this dress," Chisato had answered, with her black
eyes just like Matsue's.

The teacher did not feel like asking Misako about
the girl now. But there was something else she had
to ask about.

"What I want to know is how Fujiko's getting along.
Does anybody know?"

Misako answered with the same expression on her
face which she had shown, when talking about Matsue.
"She's the one we completely lost track of. During
the war, we heard she had been lucky enough to be
bought out by one of the nouveau riche, but he must
have been a war-made millionaire, so I doubt if she's
still well off." She was unconsciously showing her

superiority complex. As though deliberately looking away from this and also from the misfortune of Matsue and Fujiko, who seemed to be following stormy paths, Mrs. Oishi hung her head and muttered as if to herself: " We'll have a chance to meet people who are alive, but not people who are dead."

Misako was touched and lowered her voice : " That's right. As the song goes, ' Dead trees bear neither flowers nor fruit. . . . ' Did you know Kotoe died ? "

The teacher merely nodded. Misako went on to ask, " Did you hear about Sonki ? "

Mrs. Oishi nodded in the same way. Again, her eyes filled with tears. She remembered how much she had cried with Sanae when the latter told her that Isokichi had been released from military service on losing his eyesight. The sorrow of that day still remained deep in her heart. When she visited Isokichi, Sanae had said, he had muttered discouragedly, with his head bending almost as low as his knees, that he would rather have died. Mrs. Oishi had cried then, for she had sympathized with the boy, who, despite his primary wish to be a pawn shop clerk, had been obliged to return to his poverty-stricken home to find himself in an awkward position. But she no longer felt that way, for she had heard, much to her relief, that Isokichi, hard as it was to start so late, had apprenticed himself to a masseur in town. " How

would he follow the only way of living left for him
in the dark?" she wondered.   Misako, however, said
something that revealed her thoughtless nature: "He
came back alive, but what can he do, being blind?
Maybe it would have been better if he'd been killed."
She sounded as though she did not have the slightest
idea what had made Isokichi blind.   Mrs. Oishi no
longer held back: "How in the world can you talk
like that, Misako, when he's trying to start his life all
over again?   Besides, you're his classmate."

Misako was upset like a little schoolgirl scolded by
her teacher.   "But . . . but Isokichi says he'd rather
be dead to whoever he meets, I hear."   She answered,
blushing, as if she had realized her shallowness for the
first time.

"Doesn't it make you sorry for him?   He means
that there isn't much he can do to make a living.
Poor Isokichi.   Don't you sympathize with him?"

"Of course, I do.   I feel sorry for him.   After all,
we were classmates—he and I.   Still I must say quite
a few of my classmates turned out to be unlucky.
Three boys out of five were killed because of the war.
I wonder if there's any other class like that."

Just at that moment, Daikichi poked his mother on
the elbow, who was sitting beside him.   She suddenly
noticed that there was something wrong and turned
around.   Several children were standing right behind

them in an irregular semicircle, looking at them curiously. At the teacher's sudden glance, the children started running away like birds in flight, and shouted as they ran. " Mrs. Crybaby! Mrs. Crybaby! "

Gazing after them as they ran toward the public cemetery on the hill just behind the beach, the teacher suggested. " How about visiting the cemetery, Misako? "

" All right. Let's get some water first." Misako stood up quickly and ran to the house by the roadside. Shortly afterward, as they saw her coming out with a bucket, Mrs. Oishi said to her son, nodding toward the cemetery: " It won't take us more than ten minutes or so. Will you wait for me? I'm going to visit the graves of my former pupils. You may come with us if you want to."

Leaving Daikichi behind, looking somewhat dissatisfied, the two women walked along side by side.

" My, you've grown so tall, Misako! Weren't you the shortest child in my class? "

" No, Kotoe was the shortest, and I was next. . . . That's Kotoe's grave, Mrs. Oishi."

The grave was a few steps off the roadside. Under a small, discolored and weather-beaten wooden roof was a small, equally dark and dirty mortuary tablet lying on its side. In a cup which Kotoe may have used while alive, remained some muddy water, half dried up. While Misako filled the cup up to the brim, Mrs. Oishi picked up the tablet and held it to her breast. It was all that was left to prove Kotoe's former existence. The inscription read: " Secular name: Kotoe—Age of death: 20." Oh, poor girl, thought the teacher, her life had been so unhappy and short. She had completely given up her hope of getting medical treatment and even of being taken care of by her family, and had died unnoticed, all alone in a corner of the storeroom.

" My father always complains about my not being a boy. Because I am not a boy, my mother is having a hard time. . . . " Mrs. Oishi could picture the face of Kotoe, who, when a sixth grader, had said so as if it had been her own or her mother's fault that she had not been born a boy. But even if she had been born a boy as she had desired, she might have died young just the same and been buried in the soldiers' cemetery by now, thought the teacher. Tears came to her eyes again.

" Go away! Don't hang around so curiously! " scolded Misako, which made the teacher realize that she was being looked at.

" They must really think this time that I'm Mrs. Crybaby," she smiled. Also smiling, Misako handed her the dipper as if to urge her. " Here's some water to pour, Mrs. Oishi." She must have been offering a bunch of spindle blossoms; a small heap of green leaves was stuck in the cup.

The soldiers' cemetery was on the top of the hill. The tombstones there were arranged in order of age —the Sino-Japanese War, the Russo-Japanese War, the China incident, and so on. After them came new graves which had only wooden posts on them; some of them had decayed or lay on the ground. Among them, however, the graveposts of Nita, Ta-keichi, and Tadashi still stood new and erect. The confusion of the time was reflected here, too, and it was obvious that people were even neglecting to offer flowers in front of the graves of these youths who, Mrs. Oishi felt, had been involved innocently and died. The afternoon sun shone on some camellia sprays, completely dead and withered, which stuck out of flower vases in front of some of the tombs. Although the cemetery for soldiers was new and clearly marked, today people could not even afford to build tombstones to comfort themselves. It touched Mrs. Oishi's heart. Thinking of her husband's grave which was equally plain, she picked dandelions and violets from among the flowers that had just come out here and there, and offered them before the graves. Then she and Misako left the cemetery quietly. She was no longer crying, and yet the children following them called out " Mrs. Crybaby ! " once again.

Promptly Mrs. Oishi turned around and replied
" YES ! "

Misako was not the only one who was surprised.
While the children laughed loudly behind her, the
teacher said to Misako, who still did not seem to
know. " I seem to have gotten a funny nickname.
It's ' Mrs. Crybaby ' this time."

One morning early in May, when the fragrance of
young leaves was in the air, Mrs. Oishi was met, as
she was going through the school gate, by Katsuko
Nishimura, the first grade girl, who seemed to have
been waiting for her.

" A letter for you, Mrs. Oishi." Katsuko held it
out proudly. It read: " Sunday is your only day
off, so you must have a lot to do at home. But we
sincerely hope you can come to our party this coming
Sunday. Before we had a chance to find out what
day would be convenient for you, the wheat gradually
ripened, and the wheat harvest approached. Since
it seemed to us that we might miss a chance to get together otherwise, we made the whole arrangement in
a hurry. Most of our classmates are expected to show
up, so will you please be good enough to come, too?
. . . " It was an invitation to the party Misako had
mentioned previously. Among the signatures were
found Misako's and Masuno's, but it was obvi-

ous from the beginning that the whole letter had been
written by Sanae. When she had finished reading it,
Mrs. Oishi said to Katsuko, " Please tell your mother
that my answer is ' Yes.' Do you understand? Just
tell her ' Yes.' "

When she sat down at her desk, however, she muttered to herself, " Now, what shall I do? " For she
had promised her sons on the previous night to hold
the first anniversary of Yatsu's death two days from
today, which would fall on Sunday, although it was
still months before the real anniversary. When she
announced she would make *inarizushi** for the occasion,
Namiki had shouted for joy with his whole body, and
Daikichi had said with big-brotherly prudence :

" Let's offer some *inarizushi* to Yatsu's grave, Mother.
I'll get some fried bean curd at the black market in K-
Town on my way home from school tomorrow. How
many pieces of bean curd shall I buy, Mother? Do
I have to take some beans to buy bean curd at the
black market, too, Mother? How many cups of beans
will I need? Shall we start polishing rice in the bottle
today, Mother? "

It was Daikichi's habit to repeat " Mother " whenever he got excited. He must have been happy
indeed. How disappointed they would be if she

---

* Fried bean curd stuffed with boiled rice.

said she was going to postpone the occasion, thought the mother. In view of the times, she had not thought of inviting guests or procuring the priest for the anniversary. She had made the plan, so to speak, partly in order to thank her sons for taking charge of the house while she was out at school and for giving her rides to and from school, and partly in order to celebrate in a small way her first salary in many years. She had associated the occasion with Yatsu, because she had been reminded of her every time she saw the first graders Yatsu's age, and also because the graves of her former pupils which she had visited with Misako had reminded her even more of her daughter's death.

That day, after she arrived home, she began to explain to her children: " Listen, boys, I'm in trouble. The thing is I've got something else I must do this Sunday. Shall we not put off Yatsu's anniversary for a week? "

" Never! "

" Never! " The boys protested violently.

" I see. But I'm in a real fix. My former pupils are going to have a welcome party for me. They're going to welcome me, do you see? How can I turn down their invitation? "

" I won't have it. You promised us, Mother."
Namiki, who very often had to stay home 'all alone,

retorted vigorously. Daikichi remained silent, as might be expected of an older brother, but his face showed clearly how disappointed he was.

"I know. That's why I'm in trouble. You must think this over with me, both of you. Would you really like me to stay home instead of going to the party?" Then she read the letter to them. They were looking at each other silently. After a while, Namiki murmured discontentedly, "You promised us first. So you must keep your promise to us. That's democracy."

"Democracy" made the mother burst into laughter. At the same time, an idea came into her head. "Well, then, how about this? We have to put off Yatsu's anniversary anyway, but to make up for it, let's take a picnic to the principal village this Sunday. My party will be at Suigetsuro—you know the restaurant run by Masuno Kagawa, one of my former pupils? Until the party is over, you two can play near the shrine or temple there. Eat your lunch at the pier or somewhere. Oh, that reminds me. If you take rods along and fish at the pier, it'll be lots of fun. What do you think?"

"Boy! What a good idea!" Again, Namiki shouted for joy first; Daikichi nodded with a smile, indicating his consent.

On Sunday it was cloudy in the morning. The cloudy weather, if it only did not bring rain, was all the more favorable for the two-and-a-half-mile walk from the Pine Tree. The party was scheduled for one o'clock, so the family left their home early, about twelve. They started walking on the road toward the principal village which it used to take the bus only about fifteen minutes to reach.

The family had rarely gone out together, so people they met invariably asked them, "Where are you all going together?"

It was always Namiki who answered. "We're going on a peekneek," he would say a little jokingly. He purposely said "peekneek," meaning "picnic," but no one could make it out. However, no one asked again, either. For the two boys it was extremely funny. Every time they spotted an acquaintance of theirs coming their way, they would whisper "Where are you all going together?" in a low voice audible just to the family. Invariably it turned out that their guess had been right.

"Where are you all going together?" Their acquaintance would ask.

"We're going on a peekneek," Namiki would answer very quickly and hurry past. Daikichi would run after him; they would squat and giggle. They had never had an experience like this, so they felt exhilarated.

After repeating the same thing over and over again, they gradually ceased to meet their acquaintances; by that time they had already approached the neighboring town. As they were nearing the place where they were to part from their mother, the brothers, who had been so happy and gay, appeared a little anxious and asked her alternately.

"Mother, what shall we do if our picnic is over earlier than your party?"

"Then go to the beach below Suigetsuro Restaurant and play there, throwing pebbles or something."

"And if village boys come and do something nasty to us?"

"Do something nasty in return, Namiki."

"Suppose they're stronger than we are!"

"You coward! Howl in a loud voice."

"They'll laugh at us."

"Sure they will. If I hear you howl, I'll look out the window upstairs and laugh and clap my hands."

"Do you think you can see the beach from the room where you're going to have the party?"

"I guess so."

"Will you look out the window from time to time then?"

"Okay, I'll look out and wave my hand."

"Then maybe they'll think we're Mrs. Oishi's children and won't do nasty things to us."

On hearing Namiki refer to her as Mrs. Oishi, the mother grinned involuntarily. " Oh dear, do you call me Mrs. Oishi? " She almost told him she was called Mrs. Crybaby at the cape village, but held back. They had just arrived at the fork where the boys were to start climbing the hill for the shrine. When they had gone about twenty yards, Daikichi called, " Mother, what shall we do if it begins raining? "

" Silly boys! Think for yourselves."

Suigetsuro was only a little less than ten minutes away now. As she was going straight on, she saw Sanae and Misako running toward her like children.

" Mrs. Oishi! " Without greeting her properly, they clung to the teacher on both sides.

" Someone you haven't seen for a long time is here. Guess who," said Sanae.

" Someone I haven't seen for a long time? "

" If you can guess right on the first try, we'll trust you from now on. Won't we, Misako? " Sanae and Misako nodded and smiled at each other mischievously.

" Don't scare me. Whether you'll trust me or not depends on this? Well, let me see. . . . Someone I haven't seen for a long time? . . . Oh, I've got it. There must be two people. Fujiko and Matchan? "

" Golly, what shall I do? " shouted Sanae like a child.

" Did I guess right? Did both of them come? "

"No, just one. Just one. Can you guess? Gosh, you must know now. She's right there."

They had just arrived at the restaurant. In the hall, other classmates, with Kotsuru and Masuno in the middle, were standing in a row; perhaps they had been watching the three women approaching. Mrs. Oishi was surprised at the sight of Isokichi who wore dark glasses. Just at that moment, one of the women suddenly clung to her shoulder and burst into tears. She was the one in a peculiarly chic kimono who had been standing by Masuno's side. Before she said, "I'm Matsue, Mrs. Oishi," the teacher had already recognized her.

"My, you are someone I haven't seen for a long time. How nice to see you again, Matchan. How really nice! Thank you for coming."

Matsue answered, sobbing, "I received a letter from Masuno. I thought I'd be left out the rest of my life if I missed this chance. So I put aside all my shame and hurried here. Please forgive me, Mrs. Oishi." Then she completely abandoned her pride and burst out crying. On seeing this, Masuno pulled her playfully by the back hair and said, "Listen, Matchan, don't monopolize our teacher. Now, let's stop this and go upstairs, shall we not?"

They were to go up to the room facing the sea as the teacher had expected.

" Hello, Sonki." She wanted to take Isokichi by the hand and lead him upstairs.

" Oh, Mrs. Oishi, it's a long time since we met last."

" It's seven years."

" Yes, isn't it? I've changed since then." Isokichi stood still, with his head down, but instantly he started going up the stairs side by side with the teacher, who led him by the hand.

The cloudy sky had cleared up a little, and the midday sun was glaring down on the sea. It was almost too bright on that side, while, strangely enough, from the window facing the hills to the north, the sky looked as if it were going to rain any minute. The two eight-mat rooms opening into each other, however, were filled with a refreshing breeze which seemed to permeate pleasantly through the skin.

" My, what a splendid view! Look! . . . " Kotsuru turned around by the hand rail, calling to no one in particular. But she suddenly held a hand over her mouth and became silent; for she had noticed Isokichi. As if to wipe out the awkward situation immediately, Masuno spoke in that rich voice of hers:

" Come now, Mrs. Oishi. Please sit next to Sonki. You sit on this side, Matchan. Talk to Mrs. Oishi as much as you please from both sides, Sonki and Matchan. The rest of you may sit anywhere you like." Masuno sounded quite casual, and yet the teacher could sense the warm sympathy hidden behind her arrangement.

"We mean this party to be shared by all of us. That's why . . . " There Masuno took a quick glance at Isokichi, and, without finishing her sentence again, pointed at the alcove where the Pine Tree picture put in a postcard-sized frame stood leaning against a carved wooden ox.

Sanae opened the party with a brief but formal speech. Again Masuno followed promptly, saying, "Let's all be informal now as if we were first graders again. How about it, Sonki?"

Isokichi, who was sitting straight, rubbed his knees, smiling. Matsue, who had been anxiously waiting for a chance to speak to the teacher for some time, sidled up to her and said, peering at her face: "I'm glad Chisato's in your class. You don't know how happy I was when I heard it. I'm so ashamed of my past that I can hardly sit in front of you this way. But however much you may despise me, I've never forgotten you. I still treasure that lunch box." With that, she held a handkerchief up to her eyes. On seeing this, Masuno interrupted. "What are you grumbling about, Matchan? You haven't had a drop of saké yet. Stop grumbling. You shouldn't talk that way to Mrs. Oishi. Talk about the good old days!" She patted Matsue on the shoulder. The latter took her words seriously but spoke more gayly than before. "That's what I'm doing. Isn't that right, Mrs. Oishi? During the war I put that lunch box in our air-raid shelter to protect it. I don't want to give it even to my daughter. It has been my treasure. I brought it today, with my share of rice in it."

On hearing this, Kichiji muttered, "That reminds me," and took out of a pocket of his khaki suit a small cloth bag. "This is my rice," he said and handed it to Masuno.

"You didn't have to do this, Kitchin. You brought us some fish, you know."

"Each of them seems to be contributing something to the party," thought Mrs. Oishi. At the same time, she was anxious to listen to Matsue; for she wondered what lunch box Matsue was talking about. "What does she mean by 'a precious lunch box she even sheltered from air raids'?" the teacher asked herself. She had completely forgotten about the lunch box with the lily.

"What lunch box do you mean, Matchen?" she asked in a low voice.

Matsue exclaimed, "Don't you remember? I'll bring it then." With resounding footsteps she rushed downstairs and came running back immediately. Showing the empty lunch box to everyone, she said,

" Look ! Mrs. Oishi gave this to me when I became a fifth grader. How do you like that? "

Everyone laughed. " I'm disappointed in you, Mrs. Oishi. I didn't know you favored Matchen like that. I really didn't know," protested Masuno, which caused another roar of laughter. The teacher, however, looked on with tearful eyes.

She had recognized the lunch box at once. She remembered that Matsue had not had a chance to bring that box to school; she also remembered that Matsue, at the time of the excursion, had been found shouting " One tempura ! " in that small restaurant near the pier. Those past memories of Matsue came back afresh to Mrs. Oishi's mind, identifying themselves with the same person who sat in front of her right now. " Poor Matsue ! " thought the teacher. " She was so unhappy, and she seems to think meanly of herself as if she should be ashamed of her unfortunate past."

The food began to be served intermittently, and Matsue stood up quickly. With bottles of beer and pop in her hands, she walked around, filling the glasses skillfully. After glancing about to see that all was ready, Masuno proposed : " Now, let's drink to the health of our teacher ! " Masuno was the first to empty her glass ; she instantly consumed another after Matsue poured it for her. Then she sighed deeply : " Oh, I wish Nita and Tanko were here. Then we could ask for nothing more—right, Mrs. Oishi? Sonki, Tanko, Kitchin, Nita—they were all good-natured boys. And Takeichi—after he started to take higher courses, he became a little snobbish, but anyhow he was a good boy. Don't you think everybody was good-natured in our class? But all the boys had bad luck, and the girls became hard-boiled. The same goes for Kotsuru and Sanae too. But maybe Matchan and I are the most hard-boiled. We're still good-natured, though. I think our trying experiences have made both of us the more sensible. I'm sure we can do what married ladies like Miisan or dignified spinsters like Kotsuru or Sanae don't have the nerve to do. Right, Matchan? Let's show them our spirit!"

Then she poured beer into Matsue's glass. Of all the women, only the two of them drank beer. Kotsuru had been sitting next to Isokichi from the beginning, serving him each dish. Matsue busied herself carrying food around, now standing up, now sitting down, as if this were her place of employment. Kichiji sat as quietly as ever, merely drinking and eating. Sanae who sat by his side, burst out laughing as she turned to the teacher. "Mrs. Oishi, don't you think teachers are the most useless on such occasions as this?" She giggled, shrugging her shoulders.

"I'm the one who's useless," said Misako shyly, which made everyone roar with laughter.

Masuno, who was beginning to show the effects of drinking, approached Isokichi and had him hold his glass. "Now Sonki, let me pour out another glass of beer for the future masseur."

Mrs. Oishi noticed then that Isokichi had been sitting erect throughout the party, not relaxing. "We're all making ourselves at home, Sonki," she said. "Why don't you make yourself more comfortable too?"

He inclined his head a little, and placed his hand on the back of his neck. "Well, Mrs. Oishi, to tell you the truth, I feel more comfortable this way," he replied, probably meaning that since he had been trained, when a teen-ager, to be a clerk in a pawn shop, he was completely accustomed to sitting straight. Now, at the age of about twenty-five, he had to acquire a new skill. Having reached the stage where he was not so adaptable, there was no way to tell how successful he would be as a masseur. But there was no other way for him to live. His teacher generally did not wish to take this kind of student. However, due to Masuno's assistance, Isokichi had managed to become an apprentice.

Masuno spoke to him as if he were her younger brother: "Because you have returned blind, everybody sympathizes with you, and they are trying hard not to make you self-conscious. But don't be discouraged, Sonki. You must learn to be indifferent even though they call you blind."

Beer overflowed and dripped upon Isokichi's lap. He drained the glass quickly. When he offered it to Masuno in return, he said, "Don't use 'blind' so often, Masuno. I know it well. But I want all of you to feel easy with me. Talk about the picture, or anything else you like."

Involuntarily, all those present looked at one another and laughed. Now that Isokichi had mentioned the picture, they could no longer leave it where it was, and finally started passing it around to each other. Each one in turn made superfluous comments about it. At last it reached Kotsuru, who then, without the slightest hesitation, handed it to Isokichi, saying, "Here's the picture of the Pine Tree!"

Probably from the results of drinking, Isokichi looked directly at the picture, giving the impression that he could really see it. Noticing that, Kichiji, who was sitting next to him, asked in astonishment, like a person who had just made a new discovery, "Can you see a little, Sonki?"

Isokichi began to laugh, and said, "I don't have any eyes, Kitchin. But I can see *this* picture. Look, isn't this Mrs. Oishi in the middle? Takeichi, Nita, and I are in front of her. Masuno is standing on Mrs.

Oishi's right, and Fujiko is on the left. Matchan's hands are folded, with the little finger of her left hand extended. And . . . " He continued to point out confidently each and every classmate standing in the lines, but his forefinger was a little off each time.

Substituting for Kichiji who hesitated to respond, Mrs. Oishi replied each time, saying, " Yes, yes. That's right. That's right."

As she was prompting him in a cheerful voice, tears ran down her cheeks. Amid the silence that descended upon the company, Sanae abruptly stood up. Then, Masuno, who was somewhat intoxicated, began to sing, as she stood leaning aginst the railing.

> " *Ruined lies the castle old*
> *Where the warriors sat relaxed,*
> *Passing saké 'neath the moon,*
> *While cherry blossoms were in bloom.*"

She sang with her eyes closed, as if charmed by her own lovely voice. This was the song she had sung when she was in the sixth grade as the final number at the school recital, and through which she had gained her popularity. Sanae suddenly clung to Masuno's back and burst out sobbing.